Nancy Beach is one of the most i[...]h. Her experience, vulnerability, and au[...]courageously step into their God-given r[...]

CRAIG GROESCHEL
Author of *It*
Senior pastor, LifeChurch.tv

Drawing on the same grace and vision with which she leads, Nancy Beach writes a powerful book to help women navigate leadership roles in a ministry world. Her depth of experience along with her great relational skills make her a leader worth listening to ... and the church will be the richer for it.

NANCY ORTBERG
Author of *Unleashing the Power of Rubber Bands:
Lessons in Non-Linear Leadership*

Nancy's honest, godly leadership wisdom makes *Gifted to Lead* a must-read for women who desire to make the most of their gifts in church leadership — and the single-most important book for helping men understand the unique challenges female leaders face in the church. *This book empowers all of us to better lead Christ's church!*

JOHN BURKE
Pastor and author of *No Perfect People Allowed*

Regardless of gender, the waters of leadership often get a little choppy. As a woman, sometimes the crashing waves can take your breath away in a unique way. Thank goodness for Nancy Beach! She provides wisdom, guidance, and a good dose of humor to help every woman in leadership set course with a steady rudder. She fills our sails with hope, and anchors us in the truth of who God has created us to be — reflections of his image. This is a must-read for every woman in leadership.

MARGARET FEINBERG
Author of *The Organic God*

This is a wonderful book! Any woman who has been the first, the only, or one of the token few, will resonate with Nancy's experiences and benefit from her hard-earned wisdom.

RUTH HALEY BARTON
Co-founder and president, The Transforming Center
Author of *Strengthening the Soul of Your Leadership*

Who better to write about women in leadership than Nancy Beach? *Gifted to Lead* brims with wisdom and insight based on Nancy's experience "in the trenches" of church leadership. As someone who has benefitted from Nancy's gifted leadership, I can attest to her godly character and integrity. And this is not a book solely for women; every man needs to read this book as well.

RORY NOLAND
Director, Heart of the Artist Ministries

Women in leadership will discover a treasury of wisdom in Nancy Beach's thoughtful discussion of the everyday challenges they face. Men—those who fully embrace women's gifts and those who do so with reservations—will find much to ponder on these pages. Even if you don't share her perspective, please keep reading. This is an important book that actually models the kind of wise, winsome leadership Nancy advocates.

CAROLYN CUSTIS JAMES
Author of *The Gospel of Ruth*

Nancy Beach, who is as articulate and transparent on the page as she is on the platform, provides a much-needed guidebook for all leaders—both female *and* male.

KELLY THOMAS BALLARD
Founder, BeyondWorship

Anyone who has worked with her knows that Nancy Beach "wrote the book" on women in church leadership—and now she's actually put it on paper. Nancy's wisdom, grace, character, and warmth shine through each page and each story, making *Gifted to Lead* as beautiful and rich as it is important.

SHAUNA NIEQUIST
Author of *Cold Tangerines*

Wife, mom, pastor, friend, leader, visionary, creative force … Nancy Beach excels at all of these! With great transparency, humility, and clarity she opens the doors of her own life—and hopefully our minds and hearts—with the gift of this important book.

MIKE BREAUX
Author of *Making Ripples* and *Identity Theft*

Nancy Beach invites you to learn from her journey as a gifted leader. She is forthright about the barriers for women in leadership positions and honestly shares her successes and failures. What Nancy has learned along the way would fill a book on leadership and management for women … and men. I highly recommend it.

BOB BUFORD
Founder, Leadership Network
Author, *Halftime* and *Finishing Well*

GIFTED TO LEAD

THE ART OF
LEADING AS A WOMAN
IN THE CHURCH

Also by Nancy Beach

An Hour on Sunday:
Creating Moments of Transformation and Wonder

GIFTED TO LEAD

THE ART OF
LEADING AS A WOMAN
IN THE CHURCH

Christians for Biblical Equality
122 W Franklin Ave Ste 218
Minneapolis MN 55404-2451
P: 612-872-6898 F: 612-872-6891
E: cbe@cbeinternational.org
W: cbeinternational.org

NANCY BEACH

FOREWORD BY JOHN ORTBERG

Zondervan

Gifted to Lead
Copyright © 2008 by Nancy Beach

Requests for information should be addressed to:

Zondervan, 3900 *Sparks Dr. SE, Grand Rapids, Michigan* 49546

This edition: ISBN 978-0-310-52333-8

The Library of Congress cataloged the original edition as follows:

Beach, Nancy.
    Gifted to Lead : the art of leading as a woman in the church / Nancy Beach.
      p. cm.
    Includes bibliographical references (p. 215).
    ISBN 978-0-310-28596-0 (hardcover, printed)
    1. Christian leadership. 2. Women in church work. I. Title.
  BV652.1.B376 2008
  253.082 — dc22   2008007375

Interior design by Mark Sheeres

Printed in the United States of America

14 15 16 17 18 19 20 21 22 /DCI/ 19 18 17 16 15 14 13 12 11 10 9 8 7 6 5 4 3 2 1

For my mother, Peggy Lou Moore,
and for my daughters,
Samantha Helen and Johanna Ruth

· CONTENTS ·

FOREWORD BY
JOHN ORTBERG

It's been about twenty years now since I first visited a church in the suburbs of Chicago and sat through a communion service led by a woman named Nancy Beach. I was way up in the nose-bleed section of the bleachers, but there was something about her presence that made all forms of distance disappear, and it seemed as if we were all drawn together into a fresh experience of the presence of God's love. I was struck by the thoughtfulness, openness, and depth of this woman whom I did not know.

Then I got to work with her. Nancy brought a level of leadership to ministry—a dream of valuing the arts and re-capturing them to serve the local church in a full-blown worship of an Artistic God, a capacity to build teams and touch hearts—that I had never seen before. I watched as she created transformational moments for people; sometimes by the thousands and sometimes in little groups of five or ten. I watched as she inspired people—not by hyping up emotions; not by appealing to their egos; not by playing on their fears—but by painting a picture of the wonder of God, and the possibilities yet untapped in people like you and me who are willing to serve him. I watched her create a community of artists; and artists are not always the absolutely easiest people in the world to lead. Every once in a while you run into an artist who is just the tiniest bit sensitive. Nancy led them with a level of skill that was an art in itself.

And I watched her do this in a largely male-dominated world. My own convictions, and the commitments of Willow Creek, are that the Bible, when properly understood, will lead to a church in which women and men serve together in equality on the basis of spiritual giftedness and servant motivations. But still, most of the people who sat around the leadership circle were face-shavers. And I watched Nancy navigate the complexities of those dynamics on top of all the other challenges she faced. And I, and all the others who sat around that circle, were richer for it.

I believe it is no accident that Jesus was the first rabbi to teach women, to include them in his circles, to give them a level of dignity and opportunity that had been unknown. We're told in the eighth chapter of Luke that when Jesus traveled around, he went in a community that included the Twelve, along with women who, in some cases, came from pretty shady backgrounds. Imagine in that day, a little group of men and women, mostly single, traveling together from town to town. Imagine the rumors and gossip! Yet Jesus was so committed to creating a new kind of community where it was possible for men and women to relate to each other as brothers and sisters that he was courageously willing to run the risk. And so was born a new kind of community, where "in Christ" there was "no longer male and female" to stand as a barrier that divided humanity.

This book is another step in helping Jesus' community experience that reality. Nancy writes it out of a deep fountain of personal experience. She knows the tension of being a mom with young children at home, and at the same time being responsible for the leadership of a huge ministry and a nationwide movement. It is a tension every leader who is a father should struggle with as well, but which all too often men "resolve" by handing over the majority of parenting to their wives in a move of nonbiblical abdication. She knows the tension of being scrutinized doubly because she is not just a leader but a woman leader. If she responds too "softly," will that be attributed to a stereotype? If she responds harshly, will that be rejected in a way it would not be if she were a man? Is she making too much of gender issues in any given conversation? Too little? It has added a layer of complexity to what already is an enormously complex task. And Nancy has navigated it with skill and grace.

This too is part of what you will encounter in this book: the struggle is worth the effort. If you are a woman and you sometimes grow weary of the battle, know that the church needs you! For the church to go into the future with half its members sitting on the leadership sidelines is like soldiers going into battle with one hand tied behind their backs. If you are a man, know that your life will be immeasurably enriched if you seek to include and listen and learn. If you are a husband whose wife has leadership gifts, know that you and your marriage will grow immensely if you cheer those gifts on rather than be threatened by them. If you are a dad with daughters, know how much they need a father who will prize and cheer for the gifts God has given them.

I get to have two Nancy Lees in my life. One (the main one!) is my wife. The other one is Nancy Lee Beach. For both my wife and me, getting to know and learn from and work alongside Nancy Beach has been one of the great gifts of ministry.

I am so glad you get to meet her here. God has much to say to all of us through her words. May he give us ears to hear.

A NOTE IN BIRMINGHAM

Birmingham, Alabama, 1996. I was part of a Willow Creek team invited to conduct a one-day leadership conference with a group of pastors. My contribution included teaching a main session about unleashing the arts for God's holy purposes in Sunday services. The audience was predominantly male, and I had a vague sense that some did not welcome my teaching. Although our team had just taught at conferences in Europe, Australia, and New Zealand, this one in our own country felt more cross-cultural than being overseas!

During the last session, which included a question-and-answer time, our pastor, Bill Hybels, pulled a scrap of paper out of his Bible. "A woman handed me this note during our break time," Bill explained to the group. "This is what it says: 'Help, I'm a leader trapped in a woman's body.'"

The room got very quiet.

Bill continued, "I would like Nancy Beach to respond to this note."

I gulped and immediately felt uncomfortably hot in my tailored business jacket. How could my friend and pastor do this to me? I already felt like I didn't belong and was counting the minutes until we could head to the airport and go home. And now I was supposed to address the sticky question of what to do with women in the church who have leadership gifts!

I took a deep breath, shot up a desperate prayer for wisdom, and then stepped up to the platform. I responded as much with my heart as with my head. Though I had done my share of study on the issue of women in church leadership, I chose not to argue the issue on purely theological grounds. Although I acknowledged that there are difficult passages in the Bible we must work through to understand, I focused my remarks on my fundamental belief that the Holy Spirit did not distribute the gifts according to gender; both women and men should be free to express their God-given abilities in the local church. The key moment—which evoked the most emotion and passion in me and the listeners—came when I directly addressed the women leaders in the room. With a strong sense of empowerment from the Holy Spirit, I looked them in the eyes and told them, "No mistake was made in heaven when God gave you a gift of leadership or teaching."

This book, written years later, provides a more thorough response. But the heartfelt message is the same. It is not my intent to add to the many volumes that explore the issue of women leaders and teachers by unpacking the biblical texts. While I commend such books as essential for our understanding—and recognize that many readers may be looking for a defense of my position in this book—I am neither a scholar nor a theologian. In appendix 1 (page 181), I recommend for thorough study several books that explore this vital question from a variety of viewpoints. I strongly urge all leaders to keep an open mind as they attempt to develop a clear position that can be articulated, defended, and advocated.

No mistake was made in heaven when God gave you a gift of leadership or teaching.

As a woman who has navigated the real world of leadership and teaching in the church for over thirty years, I hope this book connects with women leaders and the men who want to understand them better. This objective was even part of my writing process. Each time I sat down to write at the local Panera Bread or Caribou Coffee (I switched up the location every other day), I imagined myself sitting across from a woman leader, enjoying cups of tea or coffee and talking about our experiences. With real-life women in mind, I set out to pull back the curtain and reveal the highs and lows and unique challenges I have faced as a leader, with the hope that my story is one other women can relate to and be encouraged by.

If you are a male leader taking the time to read this book, I commend you for your obvious willingness to better understand the women in your church, perhaps even for the sake of your own wife or daughters. If you only skim most of the chapters, please pay close attention to chapter 7, which was written especially for you. And thank you for your courage.

In one of my favorite films, *Shadowlands*, the actor playing C. S. Lewis says these profound words: "We read so that we know we are not alone." If this book can help any woman, young or old, feel less alone, I consider it more than worth the effort. I dedicate my efforts especially to the next generation of women leaders and teachers as they seek to forge their identities as women who long to fully express their gifts in the local church, and to reach the full potential of all God designed them to be.

May this book encourage you on your path and let you know that others who have gone before you do "get it" and cheer you on from the grandstands.

· One ·

God Didn't Make
a Mistake

Standing in the concrete alleyway that bordered the backyard of our three-bedroom Cape Cod home, I gazed intently at the back of the house. Wearing long red shorts I called "pedal pushers" and flip-flops I called "thongs," the dense humidity of a lazy Chicago summer afternoon hung heavy in the air.

From my position in the alley, I could easily observe the backyard of our neighbors on the left, the Johnsons, whose light yellow brick ranch anchored the corner of our suburban street. On the right stood the perfectly square block of freshly mown grass that made up my best friend Janet's backyard. This is where we staged a three-ring circus, played endless games of Red Rover and Mother May I, and where my loud voice (some described it as "bossy") rallied to create all kinds of adventures and productions. However, on this day I stood alone, quiet and unusually reflective for a ten-year-old who liked to talk a lot. For a few brief moments, I stepped outside the skinny, straight-haired little girl I was in the late 1960s and flashed forward to my future.

I want my life to be different from the lives of my mother and the other moms in this neighborhood. They clean their houses and take care of their children, waiting until 5:30 when all the husbands drive up the driveways. Is there something wrong with me for being a girl and not really wanting the same kind of life? I love my mom, but I sense that maybe there could be something different for me, and I'm determined to find out. I am smart, and the other kids around here seem to follow me, and I have lots of ideas. I will somehow make a difference in this world. I will, I will, I will.

My defining moment of determination was interrupted by the call of my friend Janet, waving me over to play. We returned to our usual summer spot on her concrete stoop and tried to decide what to do next.

"What do you want to do?" one of us would ask.

"I don't know. What do you want to do?" came the inevitable reply.

Oh, the bliss of such unscheduled time just ripe for that next creative outburst! I returned to the rhythm of play and fun that marked the hot and humid summers of my childhood, protecting in my heart the questions I wrestled with in the alley.

Decades later, I now see that my mother was part of a generation that prescribed a distinctly bordered role for her, with nowhere near the options I would eventually embrace. She was really no different from all the other homemakers who lived in the houses on Prospect Avenue. While my mom didn't excel at cooking, sewing, or other domestic tasks, she made a loving home for her family. During grammar school, my sister, brother, and I walked home each day for a leisurely lunch. Mom made us tomato soup and grilled cheese sandwiches that warmed our stomachs while she read stories to us. We'd beg for just one more chapter, filled with the suspense of how the story would turn out, before skipping back to school for the afternoon. Mom was *always there*, and now as I look back, I see how I came to depend on her comforting presence.

As a young woman who grew up during the Depression years, my mom had no opportunity for higher education, marrying my dad in 1946 just after he returned from flying fighter jets as a marine in World War II. My mom's course was marked out for her from the start, and she did her best to fulfill the expectations of a full-time homemaker. With a winsome personality, a terrific sense of humor, and a quick mind, my mother would have made different choices had she been born in a different era. After her kids were a little older, she took a job at our local high school where her natural administrative abilities emerged and were deeply appreciated. She also has gifts of mercy, still visiting "the elderly" even though she herself is in her eighties! My mom is most often the life of any party she attends, and countless people call her *friend.*

But on that day in the alleyway, I had not yet witnessed emerging gifts in my mom. I viewed her through a very narrow lens. And I really did speculate at times if something might be wrong with me because I loved to lead (though I didn't use that word), and was often far more interested in watching the Chicago Bears with my dad than participating in any domestic activities. Deep down I wondered if maybe I was really more like a boy, and whether God might have made a mistake when he made me. These concerns lingered beneath the surface of my otherwise happy childhood.

In sixth grade, I was the first girl in the history of my elementary school to be elected student council president. Again, I wondered if that was really okay—if I was normal or some kind of aberration. Junior high and high school afforded me many opportunities to excel academically, in theater and speech, as cheerleader captain, and as a key influencer in my church youth group. In almost every setting, I emerged as a leader of the team. My classmates voted me *Best Personality* and *Most Likely to Succeed*—honors that both surprised and pleased me, because I secretly hoped it was possible to be both successful and well liked.

When I was fifteen, two new youth pastors came to our little evangelical church. Dave Holmbo was a gifted musician and an incredibly creative artist. His friend, Bill Hybels, was an intense young man who led us by his example and by his teaching.

At the time, our youth group, on a good night, included about fifty students. Through Bill's teaching, Dave's endless creative ideas, and an unmistakable outpouring of the Holy Spirit, something life-changing was brewing in that little group—something most of us didn't yet see. All of us became passionate about reaching our high school friends with the transforming love of Jesus. We prayed, fasted, and began designing experiences to communicate the truths of Scripture in relevant, creative ways to our friends.

Two years later, when I was a senior in high school, over a thousand students crammed into our white pews every week, and hundreds came to faith. We felt like we were in the middle of a modern-day miracle.

A piece of that miracle for me was that I learned to see myself differently because of the way Bill and Dave saw me. They both observed my abilities and gave me opportunities to experiment. They described me as a leader, a creative force, a person who could influence and impact others. Because they named these gifts in me, I began to stand a little taller and grow in confidence. With Dave, I was given the opportunity to create, particularly through the art form of drama. I built a team of actors and writers, and also contributed to the overall design of our weekly events. Bill called out my leadership gifts, seeing me as a primary catalyst in the group.

When it came time to structure the exploding youth group into smaller teams, Bill and Dave decided each team would be led by a "captain." They asked to meet with me and essentially said, "Nancy, you are a strong leader and could be a captain of a team. But we think, for now, those should be guys. We have a leadership role for the girls, whom we will call 'secretaries' [how ironic!], and we'd like to pair you as a secretary with one of the weaker guy captains so you can help him along." So I became the secretary of a team led by Mark, a guy so new to the Christian faith and to any form of leadership that he asked me to write down for him every word he should say to our team. I was functioning as a shadow leader behind Mark, who eventually grew and developed into an outstanding Christian man who still serves a vital role in our church today.

Women in the church I grew up in did not lead up front, except for children's ministries and women's groups. The men were *deacons*; the women *deaconesses*. Being a deaconess essentially required the gift of hospitality, as deaconesses provided food for the grieving and served in other compassionate ways. No women served on the board of the church or ever spoke in the pulpit on Sunday except to make an announcement. As a young woman with a leadership gift, I got the message loud and clear: *You don't fit.* Neverthe-less, I put my head down and determined to be the best *secretary* I could be. Eventually, I initiated the launch of a drama team for that youth group, which tapped into my love for the creative and performing arts.

As I moved ahead with plans for college, a job in the market-place, and eventually, graduate school, I continued to explore what it meant to be a woman and a leader in various settings. In aca-demics as well as in the workplace, I sensed very few, if any, limits to what I could achieve. Gender was becoming less and less of an issue in those arenas.

> *As a young woman with a leadership gift, I got the message loud and clear: You don't fit.*

I set my sights on a future in the world of film and television, thinking I could maybe make a difference for God by bringing a Christian presence and worldview to Hollywood. However, even as I studied and prepared for a career as a producer, a little voice inside whispered that maybe, just maybe, my gifts should be invested in the church. As an artist and a leader, my first take on that idea was that it was a *total loser option*! I thought only the lesser creative types who couldn't make it on Broadway or in Hollywood ended up in the local church. Add to that perspective the little detail that I was a woman with leader-ship gifts, and it seemed nearly preposterous. Where had I seen *that* work well in the church? *Most likely to succeed?* I don't think so!

And yet, that persistent whispering in my heart couldn't be silenced. One summer, as a newlywed just out of graduate school, I fought with God on our back patio. For hours and hours I sat there and contemplated my options. Through prayer, journaling, and even arguing with God, I finally said yes to the very idea I had spent so much time resisting. I accepted a full-time staff position at the church that was birthed out of that exploding youth group: Willow Creek Community Church.

My title, programming director, described a new role. I was now the person responsible for the arts ministry of the church, and every part of our weekly services except for the message. I reported to the senior pastor, Bill Hybels, and served on the church's first management team. My journey as a woman leader in the church had officially begun.

It's been a long time since I was that young girl flashing ahead to her future. I sometimes wish I could travel back in time and sit down next to the child I was in that alleyway so many years ago. If I could get her attention and look into her blue eyes so full of both hope and uncertainty, this is what I would say.

Nancy Lee, God did not make a mistake when he made you. When the gifts were handed out in heaven, the angels didn't say, "Whoops! That's a girl baby—we can't give her the gift of leadership!" Scripture tells us in 1 Corinthians 12 that the Holy Spirit distributes the gifts just as he desired. Every gift you have, Nancy, came from the hand of a loving Father who crafted you in your mother's womb. He delights in who you are becoming. You are not an accident, or any less female just because you love to lead and are smart and full of dreams and goals. Those dreams come from your Creator, along with your instincts to lead and your passion to make a difference. There is nothing wrong with you.

Just because you don't see women leading skillfully in your church does not mean that this is how God intends it to be. And be sure of this—you will be asked to answer one day for what you do with the gifts you are given, for how you steward your one and only life. You must not think you can get off easy by excusing yourself because you are female. You are gifted to lead.

So hang on, girl, because you are on the brink of a great adventure, one you can't possibly imagine right now. The path won't be easy, and sometimes you will feel scared and lonely and wonder if it's worth it. But God will never leave you alone—he has a plan to give you a future and a hope. So trust him, and never stop paying attention to the quiet voice he put inside you. And don't forget to enjoy the ride!

If you are a woman leader reading this book, I urge you to read the three paragraphs above one more time, with one important change—this time, insert your name instead of mine. For I believe this is the very same message our Creator has for you. You are most definitely *not* a mistake. My prayer is that you will fully engage in the dangerous and thrilling adventure of making a leadership contribution to the advancement of God's kingdom. And I hope that you, like me, won't forget to enjoy the ride.

· TWO ·

WELCOME TO THE BOYS' CLUB

Four sets of male eyes staring at me. Rory, Tom, Judson, and Joel. These four guys were my first staff team in my new role as Willow Creek's "programming director"—a title made up by my pastor to describe my new position. It was my responsibility to lead a small staff team and many volunteers through the process of creating and executing our weekly services. None of the staff guys had reported to a woman before. Although we'd served together at the church for years, being a volunteer alongside them and being their boss were two very different things. Yet, here I was, about to lead our first staff meeting and I knew it was important to start things right.

I took a deep breath and decided maybe a good place to begin would be to catch up with one another. So I asked a few questions to get us going—simple ones like, "How was your weekend?" "Did you do anything for fun?" "What's going on in your family?" Once they figured out I wasn't going to dive into the agenda immediately, they tentatively began to engage. I made an effort to model a level of vulnerability by sharing stories of my own weekend with my husband, Warren, and our disastrous efforts to fix our shower-head or leaky roof. The guys especially appreciated these stories of my husband's ineptness as a handyman—most of these artistic men could quickly relate to another man who didn't even own a proper toolbox. And so began our journey together ... building our friendships while learning how to tackle our tasks. Eventually, the group grew to eight men who called themselves "The Beach Boys" as a play on my last name.

At the age of twenty-seven, I didn't have much experience in any formal kind of leadership role, but I knew enough to understand how critical it was to begin well, and to build relationships marked by mutual respect and trust. Because I recognized how very much I had to learn, I asked lots of questions to dig out each team member's expertise. Rory and Tom taught me about music; Judson and I attempted to form a philosophy about the use of drama in church; and Joel filled me in on my weakest area by far, which was the technical arts.

Not long into my new role, I also joined the church's first management team — a group of leaders who reported to our senior pastor. At first that core team included just four people, and I was the only woman. These were my peers, the ministry leaders with whom I most needed to strategize, collaborate, and learn how to fight fair. None of them had worked closely with a woman leader before. In those early days, we piled into Bill Hybels' car every Tuesday and drove to a local restaurant for lunch, where we sat in a quiet corner and did the business of the church. Years later, I still remember what most of them routinely ordered. Over time, that team grew to about ten, and for many years I was still the only woman. Eventually, we added another female leader, followed by a couple more.

Decades later, I walked into an imposing conference room, a space consumed by a large, impressive wooden table and about twenty comfortable chairs on wheels. I had been asked to join the board of the Willow Creek Association as a new member of the leadership team. As I pulled my swivel chair up to the table, I looked around and thought, "Oh shoot, here I go again." I was the first woman to join that fifteen-year-old leadership circle.

In that moment, it hit me: on every leadership team I've joined over the years, I have always felt like the *experiment*, the exception, the only one who sometimes wore a skirt and who didn't belong in the boys' club. I imagine the experience is not all that different from anyone who is a minority in any circle of leaders, whether the difference is about race, age, or gender.

My guess is that many women may relate to this kind of experience. Do you? Do you sometimes feel quite alone as you chart new waters for your church or parachurch organization as perhaps the first woman in your role? Do you wonder if there are meetings you are not invited to, and roles you are not considered to be able to play, solely because of your gender? Based on the number of phone calls, personal conversations, and emails I receive from women in church leadership, I know my experience is not unique.

The Freight of Being Iconic

I recently read a striking quote by the esteemed chairman of Harvard's Afro-American Studies department, Henry Louis Gates Jr., who poignantly describes his experiences as the only black man in a variety of settings. He talks about what it's like to bear the "freight of being iconic." Those words catapulted off the page into my heart and mind—that's exactly what it feels like! Many individuals who find themselves in the minority experience the weight of representing their entire race or gender well.[1]

I wasn't willing to admit the intense pressure I felt as an "iconic woman" until recently,

> On every leadership team I've joined over the years, I have always felt like the experiment, the exception, the only one who sometimes wore a skirt and who didn't belong in the boys' club.

when I took a six-month sabbatical to rest, heal, and discern guidance for my next season of ministry. As I wrote in my journal and worked through some difficult experiences with a professional counselor, I couldn't deny the weight of the burden I had been carrying all along. Deep down I knew that if I screwed up—professionally, morally, or in any other way—others would pounce and say, "See! That's what happens when you place a woman in church leadership." I was driven to be a strong role model for the sake of women coming right behind me, hoping to make their paths just a little smoother. Once I began to acknowledge the stress of carrying out my role, I was freed up to look at my entire journey more objectively, and to seek out opportunities to share my story and sense of burden with others instead of living in isolation.

My own sense of aloneness was rooted largely in the fact that I lacked role models on a day-to-day basis. The Willow staff back in the 1980s certainly included many women, but none of them served in senior leadership roles at that time. Two women did serve on our church elder board in that time, but I was never present in their meetings and could not observe them in action. Most mornings as I headed to the office, my mind was filled with the challenge of building the arts ministry and simply doing the work of expanding our team and creating powerful and relevant church services. It didn't seem that I had the luxury of investing a lot of energy into figuring out how to lead as the first woman on the management team.

Character First

Looking back, I now see that God was abundantly gracious to me during those formative years in leadership. Even though I felt alone and lacked women leaders as mentors, I was given some instincts by my Creator that enabled me to avoid what could have been highly destructive pitfalls as I tried to find my way in the boys' club. The most significant of those instincts was an intuitive sense that above all else, what would count most in my efforts to lead and relate effectively, is my character. Usually when we hear the word *character*, we think about whether a person is honest, trustworthy, and ethical. I use the word in a much broader sense, as Henry Cloud does in his superb book *Integrity*. Henry emphasizes that "who a person is will ultimately determine if their brains, talents, competencies, energy, effort, deal-making abilities and opportunities will succeed."[2] Character is fundamentally about the underbelly of leadership—both who we are when no one is looking *and* how we relate with others.

If this broader understanding of what character includes feels like a stretch, perhaps an example will help. I have recently begun a friendship with a woman named Marlinda Ireland, a pastor who leads the worship arts ministry at Christ Church in Montclair, New Jersey. The first time we met, I was impressed by Marlinda's thoughtfulness and depth, her obvious intelligence, and her eloquence. In the time we've known each other, we've taught at the same conferences, spoken on the phone, and exchanged emails. But it wasn't until recently that I had a chance to visit Marlinda on her home turf and see her among the artists she leads at her church. Watching how Marlinda related to her team made me even more confident that she is a woman of strong character. I observed how graciously Marlinda led and instructed her team, how frequently she spoke words of encouragement to them, how carefully she listened to their input and weighed her decisions. I saw the reflection of Marlinda's character in the culture she has created at Christ Church through the years of relational investment she has made there. We cannot separate how a person relates to others from our fundamental understanding of character.

Above all else, what would count most in my efforts to lead and relate effectively, is my character.

Much has been written in recent years about the need for emotional and relational intelligence in all of our working relationships. Studies show that these skills are the greater determinants for long-term success over all other traits, in every field. While we may wish it didn't matter so much, here's the truth—leaders are supported and followed when they are more *likable*—trustworthy, warm, and enjoyable to be around. This is true for both men and women.

When it comes to focusing on character, I encourage you to pay attention to at least four key traits: humility, self-confidence, a sense of humor, and integrity.

Humility

For a long time, I thought humility meant continually discounting one's gifts, making sure to attribute absolutely everything to God or walking through life with a low opinion of oneself. However, this is *not* a biblical picture of humility. Humility is essentially seeing oneself with sober eyes, and not being so self-absorbed that we overlook the role of the sovereign Lord as well as the incredible worth and contributions of others. I like how Eugene Peterson phrases the apostle Paul's perspective on this: "Don't push your way to the front; don't sweet-talk your way to the top ... don't be obsessed with getting your own advantage" (Phil. 2:3 MSG).

All of us can sniff out pride when we are around it. Prideful leaders distance themselves from others with an attitude that subtly or blatantly indicates that everything is really all about them. Women leaders may be inclined to express pride by wanting to prove themselves, longing to be noticed, or clutching at the credit for any of their ideas. If I feel pride creeping into my soul, I immediately do a gut check to discern the source of that pride. Most often, pride grows out of an incomplete focus on the wonder and majesty of God, and from taking for granted his grace and blessings. Rooting myself in the truth of who God is—and who I am as his child—brings me to a grounded place of genuine humility.

King Solomon, a young man of wealth, unmatched influence, and power, had more reasons than most of us to swell up with pride. When God offered him any gift or treasure he could possibly want, we all know Solomon asked for the gift of wisdom. I'm struck by what he said to God right before making this request: " 'I am only a little child and do not know how to carry out my duties ... So give your servant a discerning heart' " (1 Kings 3:7, 9). Solomon saw himself first and foremost as a little child, desperately in need of the guiding hand of his heavenly Father. When we see ourselves accurately in that light, humility is a natural result.

When my ministry has flourished in seasons of growth, when it feels like everything is going up and to the right, I am ashamed to admit that I sometimes allow pride to creep in. I have inwardly convinced myself during those successful times that I am far more responsible for the fruit being borne than is truly the case. But then I typically get a wake-up call. One of them happened a few years ago when a conference I planned and led did not reach its attendance goals. I was deeply disappointed and felt like a failure. Those are the moments when pride takes a tumble, and we see ourselves once again as Solomon did — *only a little child*. While I long to be humble whether ministry is soaring or stumbling, I know my nature is to depend more on God when I am desperate. I am learning to recognize his grace and provision even in seasons of success, and to attribute to him the worship and gratitude he so deserves.

Self-Confidence

Many Christian leaders wonder if it is possible to be humble and self-confident at the same time. For some reason, we see this as a contradiction. Again, I believe we have an inaccurate view of true humility.

God expects leaders to lead with diligence and boldness, especially when we are called to cast vision and inspire people. When we look at women who lead in the Bible, including Miriam, Esther, Deborah, and Priscilla, we see God-given expressions of confidence that ushered in big kingdom gains. No one wants to follow a leader who is tentative and always second-guessing his or her decisions and point of view.

When I led the arts ministry at my church, I had to make countless decisions every day. There were times when everything in me wanted to delay some of those decisions, to collect more information, to foist the responsibility on someone else rather than to have the courage when the time was right to *make the call*, right or wrong.

Many of us also feel disequilibrium when we try to lead with confidence because we fear becoming too ambitious or somehow seeking power. I have often wondered if the right kind of holy ambition—a desire to lead and make a difference—could take me down the path of arrogance. And don't you agree that this dilemma runs even deeper in Christian circles? The godly Christian woman is often portrayed as gentle, submissive, quiet, tender, and serving in the background. All of those traits are wonderful, but some of us were designed with personalities that are marked by strength, and others of us aren't all that quiet!

I often have phone conversations with women in leadership at other churches. One of those women, Jayne Post, is the newly appointed director of evangelism ministries at her church in Las Vegas; she is also a professional speaker and actress. Everyone who meets Jayne immediately observes her outgoing, energetic personality. Whenever Jayne walks into a room, stuff happens! She is a bold, strong leader who inspires teams to set the bar a little higher and tackle tough ministry challenges.

> *Many of us also feel disequilibrium when we try to lead with confidence because we fear becoming too ambitious or somehow seeking power.*

When Jayne and I dialogue on the phone, I can tell she is trying to find her way in her new role at the church. She is attempting to be sensitive to the expectations of the male leaders who saw fit to give her the opportunity in the first place, but not at the expense of squelching her entire personality. Sometimes she wonders if she will ever fit within a church context. Out in the professional world, her confidence is viewed by most as a positive trait. But in the church, some folks aren't so sure. If a man exhibits certain behaviors, he may be described as *assertive*. A woman acting in the same fashion is often called *aggressive*—or worse. Jayne is trying to be herself in the boys' club, and I encourage her to keep experimenting, to look for honest feedback from her colleagues, and to avoid trying to change her entire personality in an attempt to match an image imposed by others. She understands that she is in some small way leading out for those women coming behind her.

Many women leaders find themselves apologizing for their passion and goals, coming across as uncertain and tentative about decision making. This is true in arenas outside the church as well. For example, actress Amy Poehler described what it was like to be one of the few women creating *Saturday Night Live*, saying, "Women are often made to feel kind of audacious if they decide to be directors or producers or head writers. There's this weird thing sometimes where we feel like we're taking up too much room."[3]

We must stop apologizing for our gifts and opportunities! We are not taking up too much room if we are seeking to fulfill a God-ordained calling—a calling which may just require us to get over ourselves, take a deep breath, and simply start leading.

When I enter an arena in which most, if not all of the leaders, are men, I have to do a lot of self-talk to bolster my own confidence and to persuade myself that I belong. Not long ago I was asked to join a dinner of male pastors while I was serving out of town. Several of these men are well known in the church world, and I was the only woman at the dinner who wasn't one of their assistants. At the beginning of the meal, I felt a bit intimidated and out of place. But then I whispered to myself, *Just have a conversation with these guys and don't try to impress them. You were asked to join this circle, so be yourself and let the conversation flow. See what you can learn, and contribute to the dialogue from your own experience.* I ended up enjoying that meal and the rich conversation instead of cowering and acting as though I was not welcome.

It truly is possible to be both humble *and* confident. God created men and women with gifts and intelligence, and he expects us to steward those gifts boldly, to move forward with our eyes on him, and to lead with the intensity, vision, and enthusiasm he gives. Even if we find ourselves in settings in which people are unaccustomed to women displaying confidence, we must not hold back our efforts to manage the tensions between boldness and grace, assertiveness and collaboration, strength and vulnerability.

Humor

Throughout my journey as a woman leading in the church, a sense of humor has been one of my greatest allies. Too often we begin to take ourselves and our situations so seriously that we miss out on the spirit of fun and discovery that makes any ministry experience one of joy rather than a constant battle. I have laughed with my ministry peers until my stomach hurt more times than I can count. The guys I work with have witnessed how quickly I am able to laugh at myself—because I so often make mistakes and do things that are worth laughing about.

About a year ago, I joined yet another team that was previously composed of all men. These four guys had worked together effectively for several years and were known for their relationships of mutual trust and respect. I knew they were risking a lot bringing me into their circle of safety, because for so long they had been comfortable as a group of just men. One day not long after I joined their team, we were in a car together for about ninety minutes, heading back from an appointment on the far south side of Chicago. We got to laughing about some of the difficulties of that meeting, and I could feel the warmth created by sharing that experience.

Lighten up and be willing to laugh at yourself and laugh with your colleagues — your burdens will be lighter and ministry will prove to be much more fun.

Then I took a risk. I told the guys a funny story that took place when I was dating my husband, a story that revealed my frequent tendency to embarrass myself by mistakenly using the wrong word.

As I shared the story, my colleagues erupted with laughter, and I felt some of the barriers coming down in our relationships. Humor does that almost every time. Lighten up and be willing to laugh at yourself and laugh with your colleagues—your burdens will be lighter and ministry will prove to be much more fun.

Integrity

In his book *Integrity*, Henry Cloud reminds us that every leader leaves behind a kind of wake, just like a boat leaves a wake as it moves through the water. The question is what kind of wake, or legacy, are we creating day by day. Cloud asks of those we have led, "Would they say that their experiences with us have left them better off for our having 'moved through their lives,' or would they say that it has left them worse off?"

Nothing will matter more in the end than the integrity a leader displays. Are we becoming more and more like Jesus in our level of love, kindness, joy, honesty, wisdom, and all the other fruits of a Spirit-controlled life? Are we willing to face and wrestle with the truths about ourselves and the realities of our ministry? It may not be fair, but in some settings, women will be even more closely scrutinized for our character, and we need to pay close attention to our souls so we pass the test.

I routinely have to consider questions like: Who am I when I am alone? When I interact with my husband and daughters? When I have the opportunity to speak unkindly of another leader to bolster my own profile? When I can choose to either care for my neighbor or hide in my house? When I pull out my checkbook and look at where I invest my resources? When I disagree with others in a meeting? The answers to these questions are the true tests of character. All these moments and thousands more add up to either a wake of integrity or a wake of weak, self-absorbed character. I must lean into the spiritual disciplines (solitude is especially important for me) and the truth-telling of some honest friends who love me if I am to have any hope of leading the life of godly character I want to lead. No highly developed leadership skills or natural talents make up for a lack of integrity.

All of us can think of a leader who never reached his or her potential because of a weakness in one or more of these character traits. In my first job out of college, I reported to a man who was widely considered to be brilliant in the field of corporate communications. He had built a department in a highly esteemed accounting firm that was unmatched in its quality of personnel, its capital equipment, and its outstanding results. But no one liked to work for this man. In fact, everyone was afraid of him and got caught up in a dysfunctional web of relating that was dishonest and put a lid on joy, freedom, and creativity. Most employees went underground with their concerns about the boss. But eventually the truth leaked out to the powers above him, and a highly paid consultant was brought in to assess the situation and make recommendations for change.

The consultant met with each of us individually, promising to keep our comments anonymous, but probing to understand our experience. I'll never forget the day the staff met off-site in a neutral setting, and that boss walked into a meeting room where the walls were filled with flip-chart paper listing the kinds of comments made about him by his employees. It felt like an intervention, and when all was said and done, that man eventually lost his prestigious job. He didn't lack talent; he was short on character.

No highly developed leadership skills or natural talents make up for a lack of integrity.

Choose to focus on humility, self-confidence, humor, and integrity if you hope to be effective for the long term. Men and women will line up to follow you if you display those traits. When you make mistakes, as all of us do, others will be far more likely to respond with grace, to help set a course correction, and to move on. Never, ever, cheat on the development of your character.

For Those Not Yet Invited into the Boys' Club

I realize that some may have read this chapter with a lump in the throat. If that's you, maybe you'd love to join the boys' club and practice strong character, but you find yourself in a church setting where you are denied the opportunity to lead or to teach. I have locked eyes with many women who feel this way; I've seen the pain and frustration up close. I have also read their words in emails and letters, and heard their cries to understand what God would have them do when the path to using their gifts seems blocked, arduous, thorny, and unlikely to ever change. Is this how you feel?

At the close of a European conference at which I taught, a woman stood in line to talk with me. With tears in her eyes, she told me that she has been given no options to lead in her church other than in children's ministries or among women. Her passions nudge her in other directions, but every time she tries to open a door, it slams shut. She asked me what she should do because she feels the responsibility to maximize her gifts, and yet can't find a pathway toward fulfilling that goal.

Teresa is another woman I know who is absolutely brilliant and currently works as dean of students at a respected university divinity school. With strong teaching and leadership gifts, she is someone you might expect to be sought out to express those gifts in her church. Sadly, that is not the case. Other than teaching some workshops and classes, she hasn't been invited into the inner circle of strategic leadership and teaching at her church. Monday through Friday, Teresa soars with the use of her gifts. But on Sundays, she has learned to take a back seat.

Sara recently took on the role of the production director at her church. That position was previously held by a man who was included on the ten-member church leadership team. However, the original position was changed when she came on board, partially because it was not acceptable for her to be in the all-male leadership group. Sara shows up every day and does her job with joy and excellence, knowing she will not be invited to join the club.

I could tell many more stories, from all different kinds of churches and several different countries. The details may differ, but the spirit of the conversation is the same. All of these women experience pain and frustration as they seek to live out who they believe God designed them to be. When they look into my eyes seeking counsel, I immediately pray for wisdom. Giving quick advice on such complex issues is never a good idea. Perhaps you can relate in some way to the stories of these women. With great care, I'll attempt to share with you what I have often shared in those difficult conversations.

I believe God guides women leaders in one of two ways. First, God may lead you to stay right where you are, leading well in any role you are given, no matter how small, in an effort to be an example. God may choose to use you over time to paint a vivid picture of the potential of women to make a difference, and maybe, just maybe, you will be a catalyst for future change. You may not see much progress in your local church or denomination in your lifetime, but still God may call you to faithfully stay right where you are.

The second way God sometimes leads is to give you the freedom to seek out another church setting in which you can express your gifts with fewer restrictions. I never advise leaving a church quickly, without first seeking guidance and engaging in a devoted process of prayer. You must be absolutely certain, through constructive and loving conversations with the church leaders, that doors are truly closed for you to lead at your church. If you are married, it's important to explore with your husband the option of leaving the church, and with some close friends who know you and will walk with you through the process. If you do decide to leave, do everything you can to *leave well*—not in anger or with words you will one day regret. Take the high road with strong character, even as you depart.

Whether God leads you to remain where you are and lead as best you can, or to make a transition to another church, it is vitally important to continue working with a spirit of grace and humility.

Change in most churches and denominations is slow, often slower than we would like. But by developing godly character and living as excellent examples of women in leadership, change can and will come over time. Many of us will look back decades from now and see the progress that has been made, even if right now it seems frustrating or hopeless. God will build his church, and we are part of a kingdom movement that is so much bigger and more significant than any one of us individually.

My own experience has not been one without pain and frustration, though I realize I have been offered more opportunities and freedom to lead than most. I am greatly encouraged by the words of David in Psalm 18:

> *You save the humble*
> *but bring low those whose eyes are haughty.*
> *You, LORD, keep my lamp burning;*
> *my God turns my darkness into light.*
> *With your help I can advance against a troop;*
> *with my God I can scale a wall....*
> *It is God who arms me with strength*
> *and keeps my way secure.*
> *He makes my feet like the feet of a deer;*
> *he causes me to stand on the heights ...*
> *your help has made me great.*
> *You provide a broad path for my feet,*
> *so that my ankles do not give way.*
> vv. 27–29, 32–33, 35b–36

We serve a God who is acutely aware of how alone we often feel and how challenging church ministry can be. Let's choose to trust him to make our paths broad and to grant us wisdom along the way. I have to believe that if we focus on forging our character, if we grow in humility and grace and confidence, one day the term *boys' club* will cease to be used to describe leadership in the local church.

THREE

DOING the WORK

Over the years, our management team at Willow has leveraged the expertise of various consultants in order to get a fresh perspective on our church and our leadership team. Many years ago, one consultant we brought in happened to be a woman. She was extremely bright and brought a strong résumé to the table. However, mere minutes into her first meeting with the team, I intuitively knew she would not last long. She clearly knew her stuff, but she seized every chance she got to make a point of her own agenda, and there was a strident edge to her communication style. She gave the impression of someone waving a banner that said, "I am woman, hear me roar!" As I suspected, the guys on the team felt no chemistry with her, and she wasn't invited back. As a young woman leader, it was a vivid lesson and I never forgot it.

With a strong focus on character as our firm foundation, we must ultimately get about doing the work we are called to do. Our reputation as a leader is forged in the everyday, often ordinary moments of conversations, meetings, and projects we initiate and participate in. Ultimately, we will be evaluated both by our results and by the culture we create on the teams we lead. We will be required to persevere and show a strong work ethic, to discover and lead from our own unique style, and to make discerning and appropriate choices as we work closely with men.

Work Hard and Earn Respect

I never want the fact that I am a woman to be the focal point of my work, and ideally, any other leaders I work with won't consider it a big deal either. My gender is really not the point. Actions speak much louder than words, so I want to focus on doing the work as best I can. Ultimately, this earns respect. If the issue of gender comes up at all, I want it to be more of an afterthought, as in, "Oh, by the way, our programming director [or teaching pastor] is a woman." This does not mean I advocate denying gender or even trying to disguise it. I just don't think talking a lot about my concerns as a woman on the team, or consistently complaining about the low percentage of women in leadership, gains much ground. Wouldn't it be more effective for everyone to see the gifts of any person — male or female — and conclude that it's a no-brainer for that individual to be given the mantle of leadership? Once women have earned trust and respect, we can address these issues as the Spirit leads us and become an advocate for other women to also find their place.

I never want the fact that I am a woman to be the focal point of my work, and ideally, any other leaders I work with won't consider it a big deal either.

In the parable of the talents, the servant who buried — rather than invested — his gifts is the one who received the stiffest rebuke from Jesus. To the servant who made the most of the talents with which he was entrusted, Jesus said, "Well done, good and faithful servant! You have been faithful with a few things; I will put you in charge of many things" (Matt. 25:23). I am challenged to look at any assignment I am given, even those I think might not be all that significant or exciting, and fulfill that responsibility with my very best effort. It is the accumulation of countless behaviors and actions — most often the little things — that gets noticed over time.

My commitment to hard work requires me to frequently assess my contribution and leadership by routinely asking myself questions like these:

* Did I prepare this proposal with passion and clarity?
* Do I show up on time for meetings and fully engage in the discussions?
* Am I willing to write and rewrite several drafts for any presentation or document, aiming for the most precise and descriptive word choices rather than taking the path of least resistance?
* Do I follow through on my commitments?
* Have I clarified the vision for my team in such a way that all of them are on the same page and are absolutely sure of the role they play as we seek to accomplish our mission?
* Am I checking in often enough with my team, so that I can objectively define what is really going on and whether or not we are as effective as I think we are?
* Am I managing my time efficiently and focusing on the most important priorities with the best part of my day?

There is a young woman on our church staff who consistently models what it means to work hard. Heather started out about nine years ago in our ministry to twentysomethings, where she took on various roles including leading small group coaches and spearheading our compassion and social justice efforts for that team. Over time, Heather also began doing some up-front communication for their gatherings. Currently, she serves as a director in our Global Connections ministry, where my husband is also a leader. Now I often hear Heather's praises sung at home as well as at church.

Throughout Heather's tenure on staff, senior leaders have observed great potential in her. Whenever Heather's name comes up, other leaders are quick to praise her. Heather demonstrates excellence, competence, skill, hard work, and tremendous instincts in every assignment she's given. I'm not at all surprised that Heather is considered one of the strongest young leaders in our community, or that she is asked to communicate in front of our whole congregation with increasing frequency.

For Heather, the point has never been that she's a woman. She's a devoted follower of Christ, a leader, and a servant. It's blatantly obvious that she should be given even greater leadership challenges because she has earned the respect of those who serve with her day in and day out. We can all learn from Heather's example — just do the work well and earn respect. A leader should go about doing the work according to how he or she is gifted by God — and this requires us to be extremely self-aware and comfortable in our own skin.

Be True to Your Own Leadership Style

Because I started out with few women role models for leadership, I was tempted to copy the leadership styles of the strong men with whom I served. Bill Hybels is a visionary leader who captures the imagination and passion of his followers with a clearly articulated vision and powerful communication. I saw other men who excelled as strategic leaders who could help us see the big picture and plan ahead; others were tactical leaders who diligently led the operations of the church with a tremendous attention to detail and to process. And still others were masters at building consensus among diverse volunteers.

Back then I didn't understand that every leader is created differently, and each brings his or her unique style to the tasks of leadership. Something inside me knew I was a different kind of leader from the men who were my peers — different *not* because I was a woman, but different because of how God designed me. Leadership styles are not defined according to gender. Leaders need to discover how they lead most effectively, and then lean into that leadership strength while adding other skills and aptitudes along the way.

My leadership style could be described by some as more feminine, which made it a little tricky in the early years as I tried to find my way. I am a community-building leader. Driven to build a team in which members come to know and love one another as we work together, I live out all the functions of leadership with that end in mind.

Leadership styles are not defined according to gender.

When I was a new leader, my male peers on the management team would have described my leadership style as nurturing. They often teased me about the "touchy-feely" kinds of experiences and retreats I initiated with my team. Most of the other management team leaders were far more task-oriented, and hinted that maybe the arts team could get a lot more done if we weren't so concerned about knowing and caring for one another. Again, I started to feel alone in my approach to leadership. But I knew I couldn't lead authentically any other way. I'm all about community.

Time proved that leading out of my natural instincts and passion for team building served our church and artists well. The management team eventually praised me as the leader whose team held together the longest, and who also produced excellent work. The joy and unity of our team were unmistakable.

I recently met for lunch with the nucleus of the team I started out with so many years ago. We are now spread out on other teams and in other ministries, but over twenty years since we began together, our bond is still strong. The six of us do lunch once a month because we can't imagine not doing life together anymore just because our paths have diverged. I wouldn't trade that treasure for anything. How grateful I am for not allowing myself to be conformed to any particular mold for leadership!

I challenge all leaders—women and men—to discover their unique style of leadership and then to live it out with confidence and passion. The church and our world need all kinds of leaders. When I see a man lead a team by building strong community, or a woman who displays amazing skills of strategy or vision, I celebrate. Being true to how God made us makes leadership less of a burden and more of a natural outpouring of how we function best. If we try to copy the style of another leader, no matter how effective that person may be, the odds are good we'll end up frustrated and ineffective. Going against the tide in my church's leadership culture was not easy, but it turned out to be a far better path for me than trying to be a female version of Bill Hybels or any of the other male leaders I worked with. I just needed to be me.

Be Wise When Working with Men

A huge piece of doing the work for women leaders in the church centers on the simple fact that wisdom is required to work closely with men. This raises many practical concerns. Beyond the biblical and theological questions of women in leadership, the biggest hot button and barrier for many church leaders is the question of how men and women can work closely together without falling into sin. Sadly, too many stories can be told of inappropriate relationships developing among church leaders, marriages ending, and scandal jeopardizing the precious bride of Christ. It's important to note that many of these emotional or physical affairs have occurred between a senior male leader and a woman who was not in the leadership circle — an administrative assistant, female congregant receiving pastoral counseling, or a woman volunteering in any kind of role around the church. Bringing women into the leadership circle raises the question of whether we are putting people too close to temptation's path — but the temptation has been there all along, even in churches in which women are not offered the opportunity to lead and teach.

Not long ago I traveled to meet with an arts team at another church. The arts leader, Stan, would not meet with me privately without another person present. When it was time to go to lunch with the entire team, he scrambled to find another guy to ride in the car with us before meeting up at the restaurant with the rest.

Stan explained that on their church staff, they have a rule along these lines: No closed-door meetings between a man and a woman, no time alone in a car, no travel with just one man and one woman. These guidelines are common in some churches that want to have clear boundaries for male/female working relationships.

Other churches—including ours—have chosen not to set up specific rules, and yet talk openly with the staff about the need for discernment when it comes to male/female ministry relationships. This approach doesn't ignore the potential risks but places the burden of day-to-day decisions on each staff member, with accountability relationships providing guidance along the way.

The truth is that any one of us can find a way to sin if we so choose. Rules and guidelines may help to prevent some from trouble, but at the end of the day, there's always a way around the rules. What is most important is for staff members and volunteer leaders in the church to frequently dialogue about the kind of culture they are trying to create—a culture in which men and women submit to one another with respect, enjoy working relationships, and celebrate the perspective each one brings to the team. In the early church, Paul instructed Timothy to "treat younger men as brothers, older women as mothers, and younger women as sisters, with absolute purity" (1 Tim. 5:1–2).

In the arts ministry I led for twenty years, we were a blend of men and women, most of us married, who worked long hours together at certain times of the year, and who experienced rich community

What is most important is for staff members and volunteer leaders in the church to frequently dialogue about the kind of culture they are trying to create—a culture in which men and women submit to one another with respect, enjoy working relationships, and celebrate the perspective each one brings to the team.

and many genuine friendships across the gender divide. Twice a year we took retreats for two days away together. Sound like a recipe for trouble? Certainly we had to make wise decisions about how to handle these risks in our community.

With common sense, strong accountability, and the maturity of devoted Christ-followers, I believe we can face the potential downsides of men and women working closely together. I look back over thirty years in ministry and realize how much I treasure the great friendships I forged with both men and women. Off-site retreat settings for the arts team and also for the management team catapulted our vision, gave us room to listen together to God, drew us into more authentic community, and, honestly, were just plain fun. But from the start, we knew that wisdom needed to prevail.

None of us is exempt from temptation, of the need to carefully guard our heart and soul from sin. What follows are just a few practical suggestions based on what I've learned in the trenches.

Maintain Appropriate Levels of Disclosure

If you are building community on a team, recognize that conversations can (and hopefully will) go deep emotionally. If a pattern develops in which someone on the team consistently discloses more information to the group than is shared with a spouse at home, that's a sign of potential trouble. We want to provide a safe place for team members to be real with one another, while acknowledging that some boundaries are necessary so a spouse does not feel out of the loop. These are highly delicate decisions requiring tremendous discernment.

Build in Accountability

Encourage all team members to invest in building one or two truly accountable relationships with someone of the same gender who routinely asks them tough questions. If you notice any team members hanging out together just a little too much, even approaching flirtation, lovingly but firmly talk to each one privately and ask the Spirit to give you wisdom to discern if something inappropriate is brewing. The best scenario would be for any temptation to be addressed and brought out into the light before two people head down the slippery slope into more serious sin. Men and women may find themselves attracted to one another—this is normal and to be expected. The pivotal question is what to do with that early attraction, how to immediately border the relationship and ask for accountability. In some situations, God may lead one of the individuals to change roles in the church or even transition to another church if the temptation is too great.

Build Bridges to the Spouses of Married Team Members

Seek out any opportunity to include spouses—and even children—in your gatherings. When I began leading the Beach Boys, I intentionally took their wives individually to lunch. I wanted them to know me as a real person, not as some mystery woman who spent time with their husband at work. Most of all, I wanted them to know that I was *for them*, and *for their marriage and family*. I realized that the more they knew me, and knew how crazy I am about my husband, Warren, the less they would see me as a potential threat.

At one of our retreat gatherings, I decided to conclude the two days with a dinner at which the spouses would join us. That afternoon, in preparation for the dinner, I asked each person (in that era, the entire team was married) to draw a picture illustrating what they most appreciated about their spouse. They were not allowed to use any words, just symbols or images. Like always, they groaned and mumbled at first because most of them did not like to draw and they often gave me a hard time about the "weird stuff" I made them do. But eventually they complied.

That evening after dinner, I asked each team member to reveal the picture they had drawn and to describe why they drew what they did. I wanted each spouse to be honored in front of everyone else, so that in the context of the larger group, they would be affirmed and blessed. What a joy to see the look on the faces of the spouses (including my own!) as team members spoke words of affirmation. The spouses' shining eyes told me the exercise meant a great deal to them, and many were choked up with emotion. Extending community experiences goes a long way toward unifying a team and keeping spouses connected.

Be Wise about Accommodations When Traveling

It's important to be careful with sleeping arrangements for retreats and other off-site gatherings. When I started on the management team as the only woman, we took two retreats a year. A generous couple from the church allowed us to use their summer cottage to save money and have a comfortable setting. Each night, I stayed at a hotel down the road to avoid any appearance of impropriety. That's just smart. I also advise care when designing activities for the group to enjoy together— perhaps spouses might not be delighted to hear that a team of men and women spent an hour laughing in a Jacuzzi!

When men and women do the work of ministry together with mutual respect and love, everybody wins.

The six former members of my original arts team who now meet monthly for lunch include three men and three women. All of us are married. Together, we have danced at the weddings of one man's two daughters, and I had the joy and privilege of officiating both ceremonies. We have also stood at the gravesides of three of our fathers, including one beastly hot day listening to a bagpipe rendition of "Amazing Grace." I can call any of these people anytime, anyplace, for anything. They love me, they love my family, and I love them. How grateful I am that we didn't allow the fear of potential trouble working together as men and women prevent us from enjoying the adventure of ministry as teammates and friends.

When men and women do the work of ministry together with mutual respect and love, everybody wins. Yes, there are risks. But the upside—if we devote ourselves to integrity and purity—is more than worth it.

I encourage you to do your work well and to do it wisely. Lean into your custom-designed, God-ordained leadership style and don't do anything unwise as you work closely with the guys. You will build credibility day by day, and the kingdom of God will advance because of your unique contribution.

FOUR

RUNNING WITH THE BIG BOYS

When I was young, especially in my high school years, I prided myself on being *one of the boys*. While I always had close girlfriends, I seemed to come alive when I hung out with a group of guys from our youth group. I was not romantically involved with any of them; we were simply friends. We spent hours at a local greasy spoon called The Tasty Platter eating terribly unhealthy but cheap food, and laughing until our stomachs ached. With the boys, I felt comfortable, in my element, freed from the sometimes superficial conversations and concerns of most high school girls I knew. The guys accepted me from the start, and in their presence I often forgot all about gender differences. We could talk about everything and anything, including our families, sports, the direction of our youth ministry, dreams for the future, what we were learning from the Bible, and lots of stupid jokes. The guys were my buddies.

When I became a professional working woman, living life as one of the boys proved a lot more daunting. I later referred to it as "running with the big boys." For many women emerging in leadership in a local church or parachurch organization, teammates are often exclusively or predominantly male. I discovered that my challenges included learning how to relate to men in a healthy way in settings where they were accustomed to not including women, learning how to lead those "above" and "below" me on the organizational chart, learning how to manage my ambivalence about the use of power and authority, and then working through the often funny and awkward behind-the-scenes moments that clearly marked differences for men and women working in a church. Some of the moments that stretch us cause us to reflect deeply, and other moments simply make us laugh. Like anyone breaking into a new culture, women in leadership are confronted with how to behave, how to communicate, and how to simply *be* in "Man World."

Navigating "Man World"

I would guess that most guys aren't even aware that so many settings in our society feel like "Man World" to the women who linger on the fringes or try to take a seat at the table. Of course, women also cluster in their own arenas that may feel quite foreign to men. But in the workplace, and in our churches, the pervasiveness of exclusively or predominantly male teams makes the entrance of the first few women to join those teams potentially fraught with uncertainty on the part of both men and women simply because it is new and different.

The temptation for many of us as women leaders is to deny our true selves, our femaleness, in an effort to fit into male culture. This is a mistake. Conforming to whatever we think "reads more male" to help us adapt is a futile effort that will come off as noticeably inauthentic and truly unsustainable. We may attempt to mimic the stereotypes of what we think of as male behavior, including a high command-and-control kind of leadership, a more forceful style of communication, and a dispassionate emphasis on data and objective feedback. Our efforts to fit in include not only our words and actions, but even how we dress.

> *The temptation for many of us as women leaders is to deny our true selves, our femaleness, in an effort to fit into male culture.*

For awhile, back in the 1980s, many professional women chose work clothes that were similar to what their male colleagues were wearing—conservative business suits. In boring dark skirts or pantsuits—paired with the ridiculous big-bow blouses—women tried to use fashion to establish themselves as part of Man World.

Whether it's by clothing style or any other means, I have learned that trying to be more like the guys is really not the point. No one should have to deny their God-given identity as a man or woman, contorting themselves in order to connect. We soon discover that we actually have a lot more in common with male leaders than we may have thought. Men are human, as we are, and like other human relationships, we build bridges wherever we can. And just as not all women are the same, trying to lump all men into one big category and making assumptions about them is simplistic and shortsighted. We must get to know individuals and connect with them one-on-one, all the while leveraging emotional and relational intelligence. No meaningful connection can take place unless and until we are willing to freely be ourselves.

Where I work, leaders often begin weekly leadership team meetings by checking in with one another, finding out what happened on our days off, and asking what is going on in each person's personal life. The all-male team I joined over a year ago meets for lunch every Monday. Often, the guys start in right away talking about sports and how their favorite teams did over the weekend. They have been surprised, I think, when I occasionally contribute to these conversations, because I do pay attention to some sports, dealing with the deep disappointments common to all lifelong Chicago Cubs fans. But if that wasn't part of who I naturally am, I would not feel a need to do a crash-course study of the sports page, quizzing my husband to fill me in on the latest stats before showing up for lunch. It would be fine to just be quiet and listen.

The guys and I talk about lots of stuff—what's happening politically, our workout regimens, how we feel things are going at church, and perhaps most of all, what's going on in our families. Every person comes from or is building a family. It's the strongest connecting bridge I have ever found that's common to both men and women. Because all of us are either working through stuff from our families of origin or trying to build marriages and raise children ourselves, we're all able to connect around those issues. Some of the guys on the leadership team have children roughly the same ages as mine. We could talk all day about what we're learning as parents, how to handle specific situations, times we lost our patience, or what to do about a teenager dating someone we're not crazy about. In addition, all the guys are married and they like to hear my perspective as a woman about some issues with their wives. At some of our Monday lunches, I offer another perspective for them to consider — within appropriate boundaries — and they seem to appreciate that input.

For men who aren't accustomed to working alongside women, whatever they may fear can be dissipated over time as they see a woman leader comfortable in her own skin, able to laugh at life, simply trying to walk with God and do her job. I am quite sure the guys I have served with were a little uncertain at first when I walked into the room. Perhaps they weren't as quick to tell certain jokes, to talk about certain subjects, to open up their hearts. But before long, the dynamic changed, for which I am so grateful. During a recent retreat day we spent together, I vividly saw how far we have grown in trust.

The leader of our team, Jim Mellado, designed an entire day of prayer and fasting for our ministry. Jim had made arrangements for us to gather at a local nature preserve so we could enjoy the beautiful forests and streams as part of both solitude walks and team times. Unfortunately, the weather did not cooperate at all. Instead of strolling the pathways outside, we sat in a tiny, smelly cabin on hard benches, shivering from the lack of heat, while rain poured down relentlessly outside. On a side table sat a few loaves of bread and bottles of water, since we were fasting from any other food. At one point, a tiny mouse scurried across a window sill, thereby eliminating much of my appetite for the bread!

One part of our day included an exercise in which Jim gave

each of us the name of one other team member and asked us to write out a prayer for that person. Because of our sharing earlier in the day and also week to week, we were well aware of the specific needs of the other team members. We spread out in that little room as best we could for time alone with our pads of paper, our Bibles, and space to think. When we got back together, Jim asked us to read the prayers aloud. I couldn't get over the depth of those magnificent prayers, the passionate ways each person expressed themselves to God, the insightful words chosen to lift up a brother or a sister. We all had tears in our eyes, if not spilling onto our cheeks.

Our bond is strong, and I feel included, appreciated, honored, respected, and loved as a member of the team. What

Navigating Man World is doable and ultimately can be deeply rewarding.

a change from that somewhat awkward first meeting together! Navigating Man World is doable and ultimately can be deeply rewarding. While most of our time together actually involves an agenda and doing the work, the best foundation for that professional labor is a culture of community and mutual respect.

In my experience in the church, women leaders need to learn how to *lead up* as well as how to lead the men and women who report to them. These leadership principles are essential for both genders, but often present unique challenges for women.

Leading Up

Whether the boss is male or female, we must pay attention to the skill known as *leading up*. So far, all of my bosses have been men, both in the corporate world and in the church. My experience and insights, however, would perhaps not be all that different if I reported to a woman. I have certainly not always handled the challenge of leading up as well as I wish I had. I offer these suggestions borne out of the trenches of my own leadership discoveries.

Be a Student of Your Boss

Each leader must discern over time how to most effectively relate to and communicate with his or her supervisor. Pay extremely close attention to your boss's preferred way of meeting, receiving information, and giving updates throughout the week. My first boss at the church was our senior pastor, Bill Hybels. Whether we were in a meeting with a group or one-on-one, I quickly saw that Bill usually liked to first connect for a few minutes with a brief personal conversation. But there were some days he quite clearly wanted to get directly to business because of everything else he had on his plate that day. Just reading the difference between times he was more relaxed and had space, and times I needed to jump right in, was critical to working well with Bill. I also learned that Bill did not want to deal with a lot of paper—in fact, he prefers none. These days, Bill communicates primarily through email, with occasional face-to-face meetings only as needed.

I also discovered that timing is everything with Bill (and probably any boss). The rhythms of his day and his week are hugely important to him, and if any of us tried to interrupt the valuable time he set aside for teaching preparation, we were usually stopped by Bill's able assistant, Jean. Building a good relationship with a supervisor's assistant is the best way to discern timing, because that individual can predict better than anyone what to expect from a boss on a specific day. When I check in with Jean, she gives me a heads-up about what Bill's day has been like, how much time I might be able to carve out, and whether it would be preferable (and wise) to wait on certain issues.

Developing empathy for your boss is also essential. Recognize that the person you report to most likely has a whole lot of issues to tackle that have nothing to do with your list of concerns. I remember one meeting in which I persistently pushed Bill to give me an idea of what he might be preaching about one month ahead. He looked at me, then held up his hand fully in front of his face and said, "Nance, I am facing at least twelve minor emergencies that must be solved right away before I could ever have room in my brain to think about a talk four weeks from now." In other words, "Give me a break!" Leading up well requires us to walk in the shoes of our supervisor, as best we can, and to sensitively choose when to show up with what agenda items. Over time, your boss will trust you more if he or she knows you are not cavalier about interruptions or clueless about the magnitude of other concerns he or she is juggling.

However, I should not allow empathy for my boss to stop me from asking needful questions and to be an advocate for my team. Because I have a strong need for approval from those above me and want to be perceived as a can-do person in every situation, I have sometimes neglected to speak up and ask for information, to question a decision, or to even attempt an explanation about why a deadline would cause unreasonable stress in the lives of those I led. A leader must not allow the desire to please others to negate her responsibility for those she leads. Otherwise, we risk looking very good in the short term to our boss while completely frustrating those who report to us. I quickly learned that I needed to develop new leadership muscles—muscles that would train me to more confidently engage in difficult conversations.

Learn to Initiate and Engage in Difficult Conversations

About one year into full-time ministry, I came home and told my husband I had discovered a new definition for church work: *a series of difficult conversations.* That definition may actually be true for all of life, and especially life on a team. We human beings have an unbelievable ability to misunderstand one another, to hurt each other in small and even big ways, often without even realizing it. For leaders new to serving on a church staff, any kind of relational

discord often seems shocking and upsetting. After all, we are working among Christians, so why can't we seem to get along?

Sin. That's the only answer I have to the question. We're all
sinners and too often get puffed up with pride; selfish about our
ideas or pet projects; jealous of someone else's apparent success;
bitter about feeling overworked, underappreciated, or underpaid;
slanderous toward coworkers or our boss in private conversations.
You name it, we can commit the sin. Once we have a relational
breakdown, we have a choice to make. Either we take steps to work
toward reconciliation—which is what Jesus teaches us in Matthew
18—or we move on with bitterness, avoidance, envy, and perhaps
an overwhelming sense of victimization. None of those responses
has proven life-giving, effective, or capable of enabling me and
others to become more like Jesus. The only way I know how to get
through a relational breakdown, or even to get over the tiny little
dings and hurts that take place along the way, is to be willing to
engage in the difficult conversations. And honestly, those conversations always have terrified me and always will. Through conversations with other leaders, I know that I am not alone in my fears.

In my family of origin, we did not know how to handle conflict
of any kind according to the scriptural model. When anyone got
angry at someone else, our Scandinavian reserve combined with
our evangelical niceness and communicated an unspoken but powerful message: *Thou shalt not get angry, and if thou dost get angry, thou
shouldst stuff it deeply into the most remote closet of thine dark little heart
and never, ever, let it be loosed.* We learned, therefore, how to pout,
how to give one another the silent treatment, and how eventually to
pretend that nothing was really wrong when in reality everything
felt yucky. When, on rare occasions, someone did have an emotional outburst—like the time I so aggravated my younger sister
that she bit my arm all the way through my winter coat—we quickly
tried to sweep away the moment and felt even worse that we had
lost control. Avoiding honest conversations about hard things is
deadly for a leader in church ministry. If a woman leader consistently hides from speaking the truth and acknowledging hurts, she

will cast herself as the victim and eventually be weighed down by bitterness and resentment.

One of my first difficult conversations with a boss took place shortly after I began my role as programming director. This was a brand new position at the church that essentially gave me responsibility for building a community of artists responsible for all the portions of our twice-a-week services outside of the preaching. In the early days of our staff, we did not have a sophisticated human

The only way I know how to get through a relational breakdown, or even to get over the tiny little dings and hurts that take place along the way, is to be willing to engage in the difficult conversations.

resources department—okay, we didn't have anything even close. So the process for establishing salaries and job descriptions was more than a little loose. Not wanting to appear like the salary really mattered much to me—because I believed serving on a church staff was supposed to be all about ministry and none of us are supposed to care about such menial concerns as money—I never asked about the salary during the interview process. I should also state that part of this apparent lack of concern was rooted in the fact that my husband was the primary financial provider in our relationship, and ultimately, what I made would not determine whether we could put food on the table.

But then I somehow discovered the salary set for my new job. And I found out it *did* matter to me. The salary was so low, I thought perhaps whoever established it was misinformed about the fact that I was full-time, had a master's degree, and was entrusted with an entire department vital to our church's strategy and future. Surely there had been some kind of mistake! But as a new employee and the first woman in a key leadership role on staff, I did not want to make any trouble. So for a few weeks, I just lived with my own inner turmoil on the issue, talking about it only with my husband. Finally, the Holy Spirit did that thing that makes conflict avoiders so scared and aggravated—he prompted me to initiate a conversation with the two men above me to talk about my salary concerns. If we listen to the Spirit, we will be guided over and over again to pursue peace through reconciliation, and that can usually happen only by engaging in the difficult conversations.

So I set up a meeting with Bill and Don. Heading into the meeting, I promised myself that no matter what, I would not cry. I have made that promise to myself many times, trying to resist the stereotype of the hysterical woman. But because I am a highly emotional person and aim for authenticity, putting a limit on the tears has been quite a challenge and sometimes feels incongruent. In certain situations I just can't help myself, and other times I walk out with pride that I kept it together and didn't *act like such a girl.* This time I cried, which really bugged me. I told Bill and Don that I didn't enter the ministry for money, didn't need the money, and would do the job for free because I knew God had called me to it. *However,* I took a deep breath, I realized that the salary set for the position signaled to me that the role—and, let's be honest, not just the role, but *me* as an individual—was not valued as I thought it would be. I wondered if the board of directors or whoever set the salary was taking advantage of the fact that I was not the primary breadwinner—if they had hired a man, would they have set the same salary? I made it clear that what upset me was not the salary figure itself, but what it *meant.*

Whatever I feared in that meeting, I somehow knew I could not go forward in Christian community if I kept my thoughts and feelings hidden. Thankfully, Bill and Don responded with grace and honesty. I felt heard, and they initiated a process to review the salary and how it was set. Eventually, the salary was adjusted and from then on, I believe there was greater sensitivity and care taken with that entire process for both male and female employees. Not long ago, Bill reminded me of that day and we laughed together, knowing that facing my fears and raising the issue were part of my journey into Man World, and recognizing how clumsy all of us were at the beginning just trying to figure out some of the most basic things.

I have had countless difficult conversations in ministry, often with the person I report to. Each time, I prepare in advance so I can be crystal clear about my issue or concern. A few decades into ministry, these dialogues still feel very risky and scary to me; but I also have a glimpse of the truth that the alternative choice, to hide in anger or bitterness, is death. All of us can get better at working through conflict and none of us will be able to avoid it altogether. It is perhaps the way we most grow in ministry and as followers of Jesus Christ, because our character is tested in the fire of painful emotions like pride, envy, fear, and selfishness. We can learn how to be *bigger people*, instead of caving into the petty, small stuff of turf wars and snatching credit, and tussling over who is right or wrong. If we contribute to the creation of a leadership culture in which it is normal to say the hard stuff, to refuse to push everything down and choke back the truth, we will model for everyone in the community the pathway to peace and unity. Courage is required to lead up well.

> *All of us can get better at working through conflict and none of us will be able to avoid it altogether.*

Ambition and Ambivalence

If I am at the mall or the grocery store and run into one of the men on my team, it always makes me feel a little awkward and uncomfortable if they introduce me to others as their boss. Part of my discomfort is with the actual word *boss*, because it has a close relative — *bossy* — that no one wants to be, and because all of us have both negative and positive connotations of a boss based on a host of past experiences.

My flinching at being called boss also has a deeper source — my ambivalence about being a woman who has power and authority. In my heart of hearts, do I really believe it's okay for the woman to *be* the boss, especially in the church, and can I handle the occasional weird looks and disapproval I may receive for being so bold as to assume such a role? Aligning what I hold to be true in my head with what my heart sometimes whispers has been a delicate dance. I have observed that many women in leadership—both inside and outside the church—wrestle with this same ambivalence, mostly in private, because we often still feel a little out of step, odd, and maybe not all that understood and wanted. Occasionally, some of us who grew up in churches where men were in charge think thoughts like: *Wouldn't it be easier if we just structured everything the way it's always been done, and simply let the men lead while the women support from behind? Why tread into this terribly uncomfortable territory?* I don't think I'm the only woman leader engaging in this kind of neurotic self-talk.

A friend recommended a book that explores the struggle many women leaders face when they talk about the whole idea of ambition. In *Necessary Dreams*, psychiatrist and author Anna Fels writes about the striking difference in how young girls describe their goals and dreams for the future, and how those same women can barely choke out the word *ambition* as adults. Fels defines ambition in two parts: the development of an expertise, and then taking pleasure in the recognition received for accomplishment. Over and over again, women from all kinds of backgrounds and fields of professional contribution expressed their discomfort with the whole idea of admitting a desire to be recognized and appreciated. Fels states:

> Despite middle-class women's steady if slow movement into new educational and work environments, by the mid-twentieth century an odd phenomenon persisted. For women, receiving attention for their accomplishments seemed highly problematic. The fact that women could become skilled in various fields did not mean that they could reap the rewards those skills were supposed to obtain. Surprisingly, the prohibition

against women gaining access to this core part of ambition persisted despite their having acquired skills—as if it tapped into a yet deeper cultural prejudice. They were now able to develop expertise, but only if their goals were "selfless." Someone else had to be front and center.[4]

For those of us who lead in the church, we may sometimes wonder if the "someone else … front and center" should be a man. This begs the question of whether we fundamentally believe it is not only just okay, but absolutely good, right, and acceptable for a woman to lead men in the local church. Many of us were raised with a different picture, one we may think no longer affects us, but which actually creeps into our own hearts and minds on occasion. Women who are ambivalent about their leadership will tend to shrink back, express themselves and their points of view with some tentativeness, and second-guess not only their instincts, but their right to make a leadership contribution.

As a young girl, I realized that God had blessed me with a sharp and quick mind and an ability to quickly memorize just about anything. That combination is essentially what is required to succeed in most American schools; therefore, I was an excellent student who usually knew the answer quicker than almost everyone else and enthusiastically shot up my hand to be called on. This pattern lasted until about the fifth grade when I began to question whether my intelligence was a ticket to popularity or—more likely—a turnoff to others, especially boys. Gradually, I held back a little more often, tried not to look too smart or mention my grades at all, and even in some situations pretended not to know what I really did know. Studies show that this phenomenon explains why some female students flourish so much more in an all-girls school. I thought I left my hesitancy back in the classroom, but we carry at least pieces of our baggage into our adult roles, and occasionally my tendency to control the perception of myself as perhaps not too bright, gifted, or perceptive shows up in leadership meetings. This is not the way it should be.

Sometimes we are our own worst enemies. We may carry around

more doubt and insecurity about leading men than the guys we lead are holding onto. Each of us needs to carefully examine what our history and experience with others has contributed to our knee-jerk tendencies in leadership settings. Dr. Sarah Sumner, theology professor and author of *Men and Women in the Church*, writes words that are both convicting and challenging:

> It is one thing to self-limit due to laziness or lack of good character. It is another thing to self-limit because of a false belief acquired from people at church. When women tell themselves, "I am not supposed to be emotionally mature—because I am feminine," and "I'm not allowed to accomplish more than this—because 'I am woman,'" something is wrong. The church is missing the mark when the community of believers conditions Christian women to assume they are inferior, and if need be, prove themselves inferior to men.[5]

I realized that if I was going to lead the men on my team effectively, essentially, I had to get over myself, stop all the inner apologizing, and just *lead*. No one wants to follow someone who lacks clear vision and hesitates on every little decision. I needed to express myself with confidence and grace, to practice all the skills of good leadership that apply to both men and women, and not act as though I were waiting for someone to punish me for assuming that role.

I realized that if I was going to lead the men on my team effectively, essentially, I had to get over myself, stop all the inner apologizing, and just lead.

If you are a woman in leadership, ask yourself whether you still carry some ambivalence about your ambition and authority, and seek to weed out the roots of your concerns. We will only move to a place of inner peace and confidence about the healthy expression of our goals, dreams, and influence if we are willing to honestly assess those inner voices and redirect them with the guidance of the Holy Spirit and the gains that come from experience.

Leading anyone effectively requires building trust over time. And do you know what I've discovered? Most men prefer the same kind of leadership women do — they thrive under a leader who is truly an advocate for them, who develops strong listening skills, who can guide a team toward consensus, and who genuinely cares about their spiritual, professional, and personal development.

I knew that my first team of guys was uncertain what it would be like to have a female boss. I probably went a little overboard making sure they could see I would not lead like a diva or an autocrat or any other picture of authority they may have feared. I was thrilled about a year later when Rory, our music director, told me that a man from another church staff asked him, with a bit of skepticism in his voice, "What's it really like to report to a woman?" Rory replied, "I love it. And I prefer her to any man I've been led by!" That shut the other guy up quickly, and I was so grateful Rory let me know about the conversation.

Stuff Male Leaders Never Deal With

If I had the opportunity right now to share a cup of tea or a Diet Coke privately with another woman leader in the church, not only would we share the hard parts of navigating Man World in terms of leading up and wrestling with our ambivalence, but there would also be a lighter side to our conversation. Eventually we would start laughing. Because after we got to know one another a bit, after we talked about our roles and some of our ministry challenges, after we felt a little more safe and trusting, we would talk about the stuff only women would understand as they try to lead in the church. So before I close this chapter, in the spirit of fuller authenticity and a willingness to admit some of these private dilemmas, I will pretend I am sitting with you as my new friend and just get down to the very real, everyday practicalities like microphone placement, makeup, and other things that male leaders, to my knowledge, do not have to deal with.

Microphone Placement Issues

Most women leaders need to communicate publicly from time to time, even if they are not teachers. Did you know, first of all, that microphone clips are designed for a man's shirt and not a woman's blouse? For some reason I don't understand, men's shirts and women's blouses button in opposite directions—men button right; women button left. I don't know if you can follow this, but in a practical sense it means that every time I use a clip-on lapel microphone, the technical team has to take the mic off the clip and switch it around. No big deal, but it makes me scratch my head as to why they are set up that way.

Then there are the microphones that are designed to attach to the back of a pair of pants. That's all fine and good—as long as you are wearing pants, or at least a skirt with a waistband. I once showed up in a dress to officiate at a wedding and there was no place to clip the microphone! I had totally forgotten about that little detail, and there was no time to go home and change. So the technical assistant found a microphone he could put on a stand and somehow we made do. Now I wear only skirt suits when I officiate at weddings.

These days, many people who teach wear the microphones that make you look like a rock star—the ones that clip over your ear, extending with a skinny, flesh-covered arm toward your mouth. For the guys who teach at our church—all of whom have short hair—these are extremely easy to wear (especially for one of our teachers who is bald). But I have shoulder-length hair that somehow has to fold over these headsets. Then there is the issue of earrings that dangle. One time I was teaching with a headset mic and kept hearing a little tinkling sound. I finally figured out my earrings were the problem and no longer wear them when I speak. Guys never have to think about earrings or dresses, and most of them don't deal with long hair.

Hair, Lipstick, and the Fashion Patrol

Speaking of hair, just ask any prominent female newscaster, business leader, or politician what it's like to have every aspect of your appearance critiqued by the general public. Church congregations are no different. They seem to have the same need to weigh in on every new choice of a woman leader's appearance, definitely reducing one's desire to experiment. I remember one Wednesday night I showed up to co-lead a service with John Ortberg after getting my hair cut quite dramatically shorter that afternoon. John and I were hosting a celebration of our volunteers that night, and John had a lot of fun commenting on my new look in front of the congregation. Rarely do our male leaders receive such hairstyle scrutiny.

If you are a woman who wears lipstick and other makeup, those pose a few challenges here too. If I'm speaking toward the end of a service, everything in me wants to check my lipstick right before going up, but I usually refrain because I'm supposed to be focusing on deeper, spiritual things like the message God has given me to deliver. I've never seen a male communicator check a small mirror before going up to speak! Since I've been known on occasion to get emotional when I teach or lead worship, the running of mascara is also a great look I try to avoid.

But nothing surprises me more than the apparent obsession the congregation has with what a woman leader wears. I really wish this weren't such a big deal, but apparently the outfit selection can either drive listeners to distraction or become a non-issue so we can all focus primarily on the content. I am envious of those women pastors from denominations in which it is customary to wear a robe on the platform — how much simpler that would be. The rest of us need to select clothing that is attractive, contemporary, modest, and comfortable for moving around. One time the small spike of my heel got caught in a tiny hole on the stage, teaching me that footwear also matters.

We have a gathering place attached to our lobby where the pastors go after the services to greet attenders. This lovely, warm room is called "Guest Central," and I have enjoyed many significant conversations and private times of prayer with people in that little sanctuary. I always look forward to how the Holy Spirit might lead in those moments in Guest Central, and the opportunity to find out if the message I delivered had any impact on individuals. Imagine my surprise when some people — both men and women — will wait in line to ask questions such as these:

- My girlfriend and I were trying to guess what brand of designer jeans you are wearing. Can you settle the argument?
- I just wanted you to know how much I love your jacket. Can you tell me where you got it?
- We noticed you recently got your hair cut, and several of us were talking about how much younger it makes you look.

I am not making any of this up. And I guarantee you our male pastors *never* hear this kind of stuff. It makes me crazy! But I guess it's part of what it means to be a woman and to handle our culture's apparent obsession with appearances, including weight, hair, clothing, and makeup. I once threatened our senior pastor that I plan to disappear some summer "to have a little work done," and I intended to charge the expense to the church! Meanwhile, I'm trying to have a sense of humor about all this, not becoming too concerned by the comments, and continuing to do my best to steer attention to the truths God has given me to communicate. Some days, radio work sounds quite appealing.

Certain Other Female Challenges

There's one more part of being a woman leader that makes our lives occasionally difficult — and so very hard to talk about. There are certain times of the month when standing on stage for forty-five minutes followed by a long stint in Guest Central makes me long for just a moment to go the restroom and make sure everything is okay. When I was nursing my daughters and had to speak publicly, I tried to feed them right before going up on the platform, but if a baby's cry erupted from the congregation, I ran the risk of leaking onto my beautiful silk blouse! During that era, I frantically tried to schedule time between meetings on weekdays to go to the church restroom or close my office door and pump breast milk.

And I won't even get started on the fascinating era of mid-life stuff, because, of course, I wouldn't know anything about that yet.

All I can say is that we can take a small amount of pride in knowing that there is a level of challenge we secretly navigate that men never, ever face. And I believe we should feel good that almost all of the time, the guys simply have no idea. If I could give every woman leader and teacher a medal for her heroic ability to simply and gracefully handle these uniquely female moments, I would. I look forward to any opportunity when I can connect with my sisters, bring the secrets to the surface, and laugh together.

I've been hanging out with the boys in various arenas and settings for much of my life. While trying to find my place and fitting in has sometimes not been easy, I'm deeply grateful for the countless ways I have been formed, stretched, envisioned, and supported by my male colleagues. Most of them are also among my most treasured friends, gifts I do not take for granted. Recently, one of the members of my current team summed up how he feels about me joining their previously all-male club by saying, "Nancy, you've really classed us up!" Whatever that means, I'll receive it as a compliment.

• FIVE •

AND THEN
WE HAD KIDS!

On a bitter cold February evening, I drove home from the doctor's office where I had just heard the news — *Yes, you are pregnant!* I suspected this to be true prior to my appointment, but in the days before the common use of home pregnancy tests, I needed to hear those words from a professional to be sure. Tears — the happy kind — filled my eyes, and just three words hovered in my mind on that crisp winter night. *And this too ...* On top of all the other abundant blessings in my young life — a joyful marriage, a growing ministry, and tremendous friends — I was going to be a mother. I was overwhelmed with gratitude for the graciousness of our God.

For some women, having children is a long-held desire and a definite goal once they are married. The question for them is not *if* but simply *when.* This was not the case for Warren and me. Our journey toward parenthood was a long and uncertain one. It's not that the subject of children never came up when we were dating. But neither of us knew for certain if we really wanted to be parents. We didn't feel strongly either way.

The biggest hiccup in our conversations was Warren's picture of what having children would mean for my ministry and work life. His image of motherhood was rooted in the model of his own stay-at-home mother — a highly domestic person who was a fantastic cook and an incredibly nurturing parent. He couldn't imagine me working outside the home if we were to have a child. But since we were somewhat ambivalent about the issue, we chose to simply wait and see.

For nine years we both engaged our professional and ministry lives with zeal while building our marriage. We enjoyed tremendous freedom, meeting one another after work for dinner, taking relaxing vacations, restoring ourselves through plenty of exercise and social gatherings. A couple without children can usually navigate seasons of more intense work with understanding and grace, making up for those busier weeks with slower times to compensate, and communicating often about their shared schedule.

About six or seven years into the marriage, as I approached the age of thirty, my maternal instincts started to surface, instincts I wasn't even sure I possessed. I tentatively began conversations with Warren about what we came to refer to as the "child issue." Most of our vacations for a couple of years were dominated by these dialogues, and I even made lists of pros and cons. We knew we didn't have to become parents to enjoy a good or even a great marriage. We both loved our work and enjoyed the freedom we had to pursue our callings without the time constraints children would bring (about which we were pretty clueless back then). Warren was not at all convinced I could cut back on my intense ministry focus to give children the time they would deserve.

Eventually, on a vacation to lovely Nantucket Island, my husband looked at me and said, "Okay, we can give this a try." I wasn't sure I heard him right! We agreed that if God blessed us with a pregnancy, I would request part-time status on the church staff. Of course, after nine years of marriage, we had no idea whether we would have fertility issues. But fairly soon, I missed a period and figured something was up. And so began an entirely new era in our lives, one that would stretch us and bring us more highs and lows than we could ever have imagined. We were older parents from the start—I was thirty-two and Warren was forty-one when our daughter Samantha arrived. Three years later, we were blessed with a second daughter, Johanna. And certainly life has been far from simple ever since.

One Size Does Not Fit All

Not only physically, but certainly culturally, it's become more common for women to make a variety of choices about whether to be married and whether to have children, or even to choose to be a single mother outside marriage. I delight in seeing women flourish in all these diverse scenarios, especially in the church. As I describe some of my friends to you and the current realities of their life choices, I encourage you to think about the variety of your own circle of women friends, and rejoice in the truth that one size most certainly does not fit all.

Christine

Christine is a vibrant leader who serves on the publishing staff of a Christian nonprofit organization. She brings skill and energy and creativity to every team she serves on. I love watching how Christine chooses to embrace life as a single woman in her forties. Christine makes her home in the middle of a hugely diverse neighborhood in the city of Chicago, where she hosts gatherings for both her married and single friends. With a variety of hobbies and interests, including travel, reading, painting, Celtic spirituality, growing fresh herbs on her back porch, and never making the same recipe twice, Christine is not waiting around for Prince Charming to complete her life. She shows up at work every day with a passion to contribute, and then fills her discretionary time with meaningful relationships and activities. Christine is a tremendous aunt and daughter and friend. She inspires me, and her contribution to my life—as a friend and as a writing coach—has been invaluable to me.

Corinne

Corinne is one of my closest friends. She has been a leader in our church for over twenty years and now serves as a colleague on staff at the Willow Creek Association. There is no other woman leader I have worked more closely with than Corinne, collaborating together on the creation of countless weekend services and special events for our church. With the challenges and sometimes loneliness of leadership in the church, Corinne has been such a lifeline to me. I often feel that no one "gets me" like she does, and I don't want to think about what I would have done if God had not brought her to my circle and woven our stories together.

Corinne has been married to Greg, her high school sweetheart, for twenty-seven years. They have a beautiful relationship of mutual respect, tender love, and many shared interests. Several years ago Greg and Corinne were in the midst of a decision process similar to the one Warren and I went through, trying to decide whether or not to try becoming parents. After careful consideration, they decided not to pursue having a child. Instead of enlarging their family, Greg and Corinne felt led by the Holy Spirit to focus on their ministries, extended families, and friendships. While they would have been wonderful parents, they decided parenting was not the future God designed for them, and they are at peace with that decision.

I love watching Corinne flourish as she explores a variety of gifts and passions, including music, dance, photography, a love for animals, reading, watching films (especially the director's commentaries), and most of all, being an outstanding wife, daughter, sister, and aunt. Her life is full and her ministry is both behind the scenes and absolutely vital.

Lynn and Karla

I call Lynn and Karla my "mom friends." Both of these women are long-term members of our church and mothers of four children each. They have walked me through every stage of parenting, taken me out for late-night movies to preserve my sanity, sat with me when my daughters were sick, recommended teachers and camps and schools and doctors, advised me on recipes, and shown up when I most needed it. One day when Samantha was an infant, I left her in her carrier perched on the kitchen counter, went outside for something, and then discovered I was locked out of the house! Definitely one of my most boneheaded moments as a mom. I could see my precious daughter on the counter, but I couldn't get inside. I immediately called Lynn, who drove over and helped me climb through a window.

Lynn and Karla, as full-time stay-at-home moms, have both been able to volunteer at their children's schools and serve in the community in ways I have never been able to do. When various forms ask for an emergency contact, I write down their names and phone numbers — and have done so for over seventeen years. I can't imagine navigating motherhood and life without Lynn and Karla.

Char

At the age of eighty-six, Char is a lifelong friend. She served as the high school girls' Sunday school teacher in the church I grew up in. Char is by far the coolest eightysomething person I know. For decades now, she has modeled for me what it means to be a godly woman.

Char was widowed for the first time when she was thirty-nine and her only child, Rick, was thirteen years old. As a single mother, Char had no choice but to work outside the home to support her son. She was a creative writer and contributor to several Christian publications, including *Young Life*. While devastated by the sudden death of her first husband, Char chose to embrace life and live it to the max. I don't know many women more fun to be around than Char. Later in life, she remarried, and after just three years, was tragically widowed again. Char has journeyed through almost every season imaginable as a woman of God, and she has done so with grace and beauty and wisdom. I want to be like her when I grow up!

◆

Christine, Corinne, Lynn and Karla, Char. Perhaps you identify with one of my friends. I'm guessing you know women who have made similar choices, and probably know of many other choices and scenarios I haven't mentioned. *Choice* is a mighty powerful word. Of course, some women would say their choices have been limited by economics or health issues or circumstances beyond their control. But for many, especially women in recent generations, choices seem more plentiful than those available to our mothers and grandmothers. Whatever the options, the most important point is this:

There is NO ONE RIGHT WAY to navigate life as a woman.

Scripture indicates that not all Christians will or should be married, as the apostle Paul chose to focus his primary energies on his ministry. We also see examples of women throughout the Bible who, despite cultural norms of that era, played vital roles in the early church. Way back in the Old Testament, Esther used her discernment skills in a way that resulted in the dramatic rescue of her people. Deborah was a prophet in her day, and Priscilla and other women contributed to the establishment of the early church. Our heavenly Father guides the paths of women in a beautiful variety of directions, including several different seasons along our paths that each call out a unique focus and perspective. If we confine our thinking to one plan that fits every woman, we limit the possibilities of each individual living out her own custom-designed story.

My Motherhood Story

My story ended up including motherhood. And after nine years without children, it was a huge adjustment. When I came home with my first child, my hormones were raging out of control and I truly could not believe that anyone would allow two truly incompetent people like Warren and me to be responsible for this tiny baby. I wish I had a videotape of the first time we tried to give Samantha a bath—one of us reading the notes from our parenthood class, the other trying not to drop our slippery seven-pounder in the kitchen sink. We were both sleep-deprived and stunned at how the arrival of our little girl had so dramatically transformed our lives.

For a couple of weeks, I cried frequently for no apparent reason. Warren would walk through the room where I was nursing and crying and say, "What's the matter now?" (He's just so sensitive.) And I would respond, "I don't know!" In the midst of all this, I received a phone call from my friend Corinne, who was in Germany leading an exciting ministry project. I heard her voice and immediately thought, "What has happened to me? I used to be the one traveling, doing meaningful work that I loved. Now I'm a fat, non-stop milking machine. This can't be my life." It reminded me of a classified ad I'd seen in our local paper that read: "Windsurfers! Had baby, life over, selling gear." That's exactly what I felt like for a few days — had baby, life over.

My husband and I agreed that after three months, I would return to my ministry role part-time, aiming for twenty hours a week. Early in the pregnancy, I mustered the courage to approach my boss and friend, Bill Hybels, and propose a plan. I would continue to lead the arts ministry but would cut my hours in half by delegating tasks. No woman in senior leadership on our staff had asked for this kind of arrangement, and I realized the answer could be no. I also asked Bill if he would consider allowing me to continue as a leader on the church management team. Gulp.

To my surprise, Bill responded with openness and said we could certainly try to make my plan work. Thus began my journey as a part-time working mom. I pumped breast milk in the restroom at our church offices and was blessed with a part-time nanny who had already raised her children and became like another grandmother to my girls. But of course, nothing was simple or easy.

Good Enough Mothers

With the wide range of options available to women, many do end up becoming mothers as I did. Women managing both church leadership and motherhood face a unique set of challenges. Many of us battle a monster that is incredibly destructive. She lurks in the hidden recesses of our minds, attacks us with doubt, clubs us with guilt, and lays waste to our self-esteem. She is what I call *The Perfect Mother Monster* (or PMM, *not* PMS). The Perfect Mother Monster is a totally unrealistic creation based either on our own mothers, cultural expectations, images from the media, or simply our own impossibly high standards. Every woman's PMM is slightly different, but all PMMs share a few common traits:

- The Perfect Mother is *always there.*
- The Perfect Mother always looks great and so does her perfect little home.
- The Perfect Mother never loses her patience.
- The Perfect Mother never misses a field trip or an opportunity to be Room Mom.
- The Perfect Mother always serves nutritious home-cooked meals.
- The Perfect Mother, if she works outside the home, still does all of the above ... flawlessly.
- And, of course, the Perfect Mother has perfect children.

The majority of mothers I talk to have unrealistic fantasies and expectations of motherhood. Many women say, "Whatever I'm doing, whoever I am, *it's never enough.*" We expect more from ourselves, or we think others do. No matter what you do or don't do for your child, deep down you have the sneaking suspicion that you're somehow doing it all wrong. You may feel like a dazzling success as a mother one day and a complete washout the next.

"Whatever I'm doing, whoever I am, it's never enough."

One mother describes it this way: "It seems to me at times as if the weight of responsibility connected with these little immortal beings would prove too much for me—am I doing what's right? Am I doing enough? Am I not doing too much ...?" That woman was the mother of author Louisa May Alcott, author of *Little Women,* and she said those words in 1883! Apparently mothers have been struggling with guilt for a long time.

I remember quite vividly the day I realized for certain I would not be a perfect mother. My first daughter, Samantha, was a fairly easy baby—no colic, a great sleeper, not too many colds or health problems. So I can honestly say that, until she was about age three, I thought I was doing a pretty good job. I had no major regrets—yet.

Then some friends recommended a book called *Toilet Training in a Day*. This strategy promised success in just three to four hours. Basically, it was behavior modification and it had worked fabulously for several moms I knew. So I practically memorized the book and took six pages of notes. I selected the exact day when Samantha would be potty trained. I was all ready to go with treats for rewards, the phone turned off, and a rested, happy little girl. Needless to say, the next six hours were some of the most frustrating in my life. Samantha taught her dolly to go potty. She loved the treats. But we had five accidents in the pants. We had long chats and story time while she sat on the little chair, but she would not go. Then five minutes later my kitchen floor was a puddle.

I felt like such a terrible failure. Samantha obviously had not ever learned about Pavlov's dog! I put her diaper back on at six o'clock that evening. All I wanted was to sit in a hot bath with a bottle of wine and cry—and I'm not a big drinker. The saddest part was that my little girl saw how impatient and frustrated Mommy became and she felt awful. I made a big deal out of something she did not feel at all motivated to change, and we waited many months before trying again. On that day, I saw for the first of countless times that I would never be a perfect mother.

Browsing in a bookstore one day as a new mom, I discovered a book with a title that caught my eye, *Good Enough Mothers*. My first reaction was, I can never be good enough. But I was intrigued, so I purchased Melinda Marshall's book. Marshall's writing helped me sort through my ambivalence about working outside the home, and my sense that I wasn't measuring up in any arena—as a leader, a wife, a mother, a daughter, a friend, and certainly not as a home-maker. Through reading and prayer and talking openly with other moms, I began to feel a freedom to reinvent motherhood for myself and my family, and to let go of my perfectionistic standards and debilitating guilt. Certainly when my four-year-old daughter held onto my pant leg and cried crocodile tears when I left three mornings a week, I was filled with doubt. But upon my arrival at the office, our sensitive and wise nanny, Katie, called me to report that I wasn't even completely out of the driveway before Samantha immediately turned to her, shut off the tears, and inquired, "What's the plan for today, Nanny?" Both my girls are quite the drama queens, and I had to learn to interpret objectively how my work hours were actually affecting them and what the best balance would be for our unique situation.

The Myth of Having It All ... All at Once

Melinda Marshall writes a lot about trade-offs and the kind of elusive balance most moms are searching for, especially if they work outside the home. She has an interesting take on the most commonly used word for describing the life of a working mom: juggling.

> By and large what limits choice for working mothers is the tendency to regard all roles as morally or ideologically critical, and therefore equally important. This is called juggling, an apt term since it implies all the balls must be kept in the air and the juggler can never rest—she is doomed, in fact, to keep everything in perpetual motion without ever having the satisfaction of getting somewhere or finishing anything. Should the juggler tire, or relax her concentration, the act culminates in failure: The audience pays attention to the juggler only as long as she defies the inevitable.[6]

Rather than trying to perfectly balance every responsibility we hold, I advise mothers to recognize that our lives are an ongoing series of trade-offs and compromises. Most of us don't like that idea of *compromise*, but I contend that all people make these kinds of trade-offs every day. We decide whether we can sacrifice the time to work out, call our parents, vacuum the house, drive a child to soccer practice, have coffee with a friend, and all the other little decisions that together make up the fabric of our daily lives. I began to learn that unless I adjusted my expectations in every area, I would walk through life miserable and racked with guilt. Every parenting expert agrees that an unhappy mom, even a mom who sees herself as a martyr and gives up all personal time for the sake of her children, is not doing anyone in the family any favors.

Learning to listen to and trust the inner voice of the Holy Spirit as my husband and I make countless decisions and prioritize each week is the only way I know to create a version of motherhood and ministry that fits who God created me uniquely to be. I recognize that I will do this differently than other women and other moms, and that is how it should be. We're all making this up as we go along, learning from our mistakes, paying attention to the still, small voice that nudges us in one direction or another. Motherhood is an art, not a science.

When Melinda Marshall describes compromise and trade-offs, I resonate completely with her picture:

> Most women ultimately seek compromise as a means, not an end. They're not *lowering* their expectations but simply weighing more carefully what they're willing to pay for what they want. Instead of harping on what they cannot change, they are focusing on actions they can and will take. Instead of seeing all options as equally vital to pursue, they're exercising real choice by prioritizing, by letting go those pursuits that serve only to gratify other people's unrealistic expectations. They don't eliminate roles they enjoy simply because they cannot perform them perfectly. Achievement, for them, *is* balance, attained not at unbearable cost but by making acceptable trade-offs ... They don't want life to be easy; they just want to feel like they are making it better. They don't want to be perfect; they just don't want to be expected to be. What they want is to be *good enough.*[7]

I make trade-offs all the time. Choosing to have a house that is rarely perfectly clean (okay … never) or choosing to hire a cleaning service to come in every other week is one of those trade-offs. I realize not every budget can afford this kind of help, and I don't take it for granted. When my girls were quite young, I celebrated the weeks I could get out and exercise three times. Now that they are older, I can increase the frequency. Date nights, time with girlfriends, overnights alone with my husband, saying no to major volunteer roles in the public school, turning down some, but not all, of the ministry opportunities that require travel — all of these add up to little decisions that collectively comprise a life. Every family is unique and every situation different. I was blessed with a husband who is self-employed and worked out of our home during the early years of our daughters' lives. He is a key ingredient every step of the way, freeing me up to do ministry, including some entire weeks of travel for overseas conferences. Not every husband has that kind of flexibility, and some mothers navigate the parenting journey without much, or even any, help from a spouse. I truly cannot fully imagine the challenges of a single mother with primary custody of her children — and I hold in high esteem those I know who get up every day and do the job with such grace and courage.

> *Every family is unique and every situation different.*

Our lives as women and mothers are also seasonal. Just when I thought I had a handle on the rhythm of my girls' schedules, something changed. Each season of motherhood presents different challenges and requires different trade-offs. I'm quite sure my older daughter will be telling her therapist someday that I missed several of her school dances and the photo shoots beforehand. By a fluke of scheduling and the lack of clear information from the schools, I did miss a few. Last season I was absolutely determined not to miss the prom, and I avoided any travel the entire month of May. But whenever I have been absent, my husband has always picked up the slack. Like many fathers of today, Warren is highly engaged and as flexible as he can be to help make our family system work.

The *Chicago Tribune* ran a column recently with the positive headline, "Hey, Mom, you are doing fine, study says." The article reported a study from the University of Maryland that concludes today's mothers spend more hours focused on their children than their own mothers did forty years ago. Although most mothers feel they don't do enough, the study reveals that in reality, moms are currently more engaged each week in both primary time (when a child is the focus of a parent's attention) and secondary time.[8] This is surprising news to most contemporary moms, who assume that their own mothers and grandmothers must have been far more attentive than they can hope to be.

Ultimately, I believe a woman who is devoted to following Jesus Christ will receive the guidance and discernment to know in any given season how she is really doing as a mom. When we pay attention to the right kind of guilt, we may discover we have not focused enough on a given area of our lives and choose to make a needed adjustment. I, for one, have decided to abandon the entire image of juggling because I inevitably drop balls and feel like a failure. Rather, I suggest we recognize that the Spirit will reveal to us certain eras in which we should intentionally focus more on our children or our husband or our aging parents or our ministry challenges or our friends. And when that era wraps up, we will turn again with energy and passion to whatever has received less focus for a time. This is what I believe it means to actually walk with God, day by day, moment by moment. Our God can be trusted to show us what it means to rest in being good enough. There truly are no perfect mothers, and none of us will know the bliss of having it all ... all at once.

I Want a Wife!

I cannot end this chapter without acknowledging that my journey as a mother working outside the home is far different from what I observe among the dads on our staff. Sometimes I've wrestled with jealousy knowing that most of these guys are married to a full-time, stay-at-home mom who frees them up to focus on a lot more ministry work than I am able to do. Without intending to be insensitive, my male colleagues have shared stories of how their wives handle the household management, do most of the chauffeuring, help with homework, and attend to the little details of life all of us deal with, like doctor appointments, trips to the dry cleaners, getting the oil changed in the car, etc. In these settings I secretly think to myself, "I want a wife!" While I am deeply grateful for the contribution Warren makes in our home, the reality is that, as the mom, I still feel the weight and burden of holding it all together.

Some of these clearly defined gender roles are changing, and I know of a few couples where the load at home truly is shared equally. In our situation, I admit that we have chosen to grow comfortable with a fairly typical division of responsibilities and household tasks. Warren takes care of the lawn, snowblowing, maintaining the cars, and paying the bills. I figure out the meals and laundry and general house cleaning. In addition, mostly because I tend to be more organized, I am the family scheduler. When Warren and I prepare for a getaway weekend and we leave the girls with family or friends, Warren only has to decide what to pack for himself. Meanwhile, I make long lists of notes for our caregiver on every detail of the girls' schedules, figuring out car pools and play dates. By the time we get away, I'm exhausted from all the preparation! Yet the raw truth is that I often take on these tasks either because I'm afraid they won't get done correctly, or because I love to play the role of the martyr.

Over the years, I have learned that the men I work with don't fully understand how different it is for me to do our ministry work than for them.

I do believe there is a fundamental difference for most children in how they respond to a mother's absence versus a father's absence. When I prepared to leave for Europe or a long journey to Australia, especially when my girls were quite young, they were distraught leading up to my departure. We developed a tradition in our home known as the *pink calendar.* I used a large pink poster board and created a calendar for my trip to help the girls count down the days until my return. I pinned a note on each day of the calendar. Some of those notes read "Present Day," which indicated little gifts for them were hiding in a stash in the closet. Before long, my girls so looked forward to the pink calendar that I wondered if they preferred my absence! But here's what fascinated me — whenever Warren needed to travel for his ministry work, there were no tears. Instead, the girls calmly said, "Bye, Dad," and gave him a hug. Our daughters adore their father, but clearly they have a much harder time if Mom is gone. This sometimes makes me crazy … and yet it's so nice to be wanted.

Over the years, I have learned that the men I work with don't fully understand how different it is for me to do our ministry work than for them. Many of them just don't get it. For example, when some of the guys on the management team suggest a 6:00 a.m. breakfast meeting, I'm the only one who has to routinely say, "I'm sorry, that won't work for me." Getting the girls ready for school and dealing with car pools makes those early meetings just too hard. Or they request a spontaneous meeting or last-minute trip, knowing that for most of them, it's no problem at home. Meanwhile, my blood pressure is rising and my mind is spinning with questions like, "How can I possibly make this work?" In some cases, I have gently shared some of these challenges with my male colleagues because we serve together in community. It may be tempting to put up a front that I can handle anything, no problem, which is actually prideful. I am also a little afraid that if I reveal my limitations, I may lose my seat at the table. But when I choose to sometimes explore alternatives, to speak up for the need of a more flexible plan, I pave the way for other women these guys will work with in the future, as well as for dads who also need to make some compromises. In this lifetime, I'll never be blessed with a wife of my own ... but a full-time housekeeper or butler sure would be great!

What We Model Matters

Whether or not a mother works outside the home, what we model is hugely significant for our sons and daughters. We must not raise young people who believe that the world is all about them. I believe when a child recognizes that Mom or Dad is crazy about them, but *also* has some other interests, passions, and responsibilities, that child is well served. Watching a parent fully engaged in maximizing his or her spiritual gifts impacts a son or daughter for a long time. For children whose parents are married, they have the opportunity to observe what it looks like for a husband and wife to serve one another, to be one another's advocate and support, and to free one another up to make a contribution to the world.

Ultimately, this boils down to knowing the true source of our identity. Our fundamental identity is *not* as mothers or fathers. Drs. Henry Cloud and John Townsend remind us that parenting is a temporary job, not an identity. "Parents who do not have a life apart from their kids teach the kids that the universe revolves around them ... Meet the child's needs, then require him to meet his own while you meet yours."[9] What a gift to give our children!

Our fundamental identity is not as mothers or fathers.

Rather than assuming Mom and Dad will always be there exclusively for them, kids understand that other people and their needs matter as well. I love to see sons and daughters who begin to serve alongside their parents, experimenting and discovering their own interests and gifts along the way.

One mom I know took her boys every month to a nursing home

where they "adopted" some grandparents to care for. While her sons would sometimes gripe about the sights and smells of that place, they learned to set aside their own comfort for a couple of hours and develop empathy for some aging people who spent most of their days all alone. At our church, some parents include their sons and daughters in caring for the church property, setting up sound equipment, or serving food. What incredibly significant lessons these kids are learning.

A couple of years ago, Warren and I took our girls to the Dominican Republic to visit some of the ministry partners our church has there. Warren currently leads the Global Connections ministry, and he longed for Samantha and Johanna to break out of the suburban bubble and get a glimpse of life in an impoverished country. I'll never forget walking with a pastor in Santo Domingo, showing our girls the barrio within striking distance of the church where whole families live in spaces smaller than my daughters' bedrooms. For at least a few days, they lived with a reality check that challenged their sense of what is truly a "need" versus what is a "want." I was thrilled to see them watch their dad in action, living out who God made him to be as a servant of the under-resourced.

Because both my girls have some of my DNA, they love the arts—especially acting. From the time they were little, I took them along to some of our rehearsals where they saw musicians, actors, dancers, and technical artists serving with humility, authenticity, creativity, and excellence. Initially, I thought bringing them to these gatherings was mostly about avoiding childcare, but they were actually learning from all those early experiences, and also building relationships with other godly adults. How delighted I am to observe them as teenagers, writing, acting, and even directing at times for various youth gatherings or our weekly church services. There's nothing like seeing your children live in the center of their own gifts and knowing what they were born to do!

Being a mom in ministry has been the most stretching, complicated, and sometimes frustrating challenge in my life. But if I had it to do all over again, I would not make any major changes. I know

I am a *good enough* mother. I have made my share of mistakes, but I don't walk through life with huge regrets. If you are a mom, I urge you to listen to the quiet voice of the Spirit and allow our God to help you design your own path for motherhood. No one can write the script for you—your story will be entirely your own. And in the big-picture scheme of things, you can give God praise as I did when I first learned a baby was forming in my womb ... *And this too!*

• SIX •

FINDING YOUR VOICE

everal years ago I received a call from a college professor in North Carolina, a lovely woman named Jane Stephens, who asked if she could spend some time interviewing me for her dissertation project. When I inquired about the focus of her research, Jane explained that she had selected a dozen women leaders from various fields as case studies to explore the female voice. I really had no idea what she was talking about, but I liked Jane over the phone and thought if nothing else, I'd love to have lunch with her. For a few hours one afternoon, we sat in my favorite local restaurant drinking too much iced tea and getting to know one another.

Talk about an inspiring woman! I learned that Jane is a professor of English literature at a liberal arts college, is married to a doctor, and is the mother of six children. Her two youngest children came to the family via a miraculous adoption in Kenya, where Jane spent six months working on her dissertation. Just imagining the demands of Jane's full life made me want to take a nap. But I discovered that Jane was as down-to-earth and accessible as anyone I had ever met. She was a terrific listener, conveying a genuine curiosity and deep interest in what I had to say. I immediately liked and admired her.

Jane asked highly perceptive questions about my childhood, about women who had influenced me, and then, eventually, we got around to the core subject of finding one's voice. Jane told me she had come to one of the first conferences our church conducted for other church leaders, which was attended primarily by male pastors. She observed me then as a young woman in two settings: giving my prepared comments in front of the entire group in a main session, and also as I fielded questions during a workshop. Jane asked if I would be open to hearing her thoughts on the differences she observed in my communication style between the main session and the workshop. Because she had already won my trust through our warm conversation, I said, "Sure, I'd love to hear your perspective."

Jane proceeded to explain that when I spoke to the main session, she sensed some tentativeness, that my communication was articulate but not compelling. It was in the workshop Q-and-A session that she felt she heard my real voice for the first time. As I responded to a challenging question, Jane said she could sense I was processing and thinking out loud, exhibiting a sense of candor, passion, and discovery, and, in her words, *becoming myself.*

Jane and I then explored together what it means to find one's voice, especially as a woman working in a predominantly male environment. Jane lovingly nudged me to avoid copying the voices of others, and instead, to zealously pursue and develop my own unique voice.

Jane's words still echo in my mind and heart fifteen years later. She went on to complete her dissertation, a portion of which she later condensed into an article I've included in appendix 2 (page 185). Her contribution to the study of how women leaders communicate, and the differences between male and female rhetoric, is hugely significant and fills a gap in what had been previously explored. Here is a fascinating passage from Jane's work:

> Since Aristotle, rhetoric has been defined as "the faculty of discovering all available means of persuasion," and the history of leadership and rhetoric has been a history of those who had access to civic authority and a public forum. Until recently, women have had neither of these advantages, but have influenced those around them in significant ways by discovering their own "available means of persuasion." Historically,

women have been admonished to value the influence they hold through relationships with a husband or son; they've lead by persuading the persuaders or informing the informers. From this liminal position, they've learned to harness the power of language in less overt and formal venues than those of traditional hierarchical forums—in songs, and stories, at slumber parties and club meetings, through letters and conversations. Thus, they have developed a history of rhetoric and leadership that has fueled the development of our world both in ways that we are only now beginning to recover and in other ways that we have already lost and will never fully know. As a result, the ongoing story of women's leadership has been diminished, not only by our historical lack of access to direct and legitimate authority, but by our ongoing lack of connection to the unrecorded traditions of powerful female voices. If we lose the memory, language, and imagery that we have inherited from women leaders in the past in favor of a masculine style of leadership, might our next generation of women leaders become what Gloria Steinem calls "female impersonators"?[10]

How can a woman leader and teacher who is surrounded by male communicators avoid the tendency to simply impersonate them? What will keep her from neglecting the discovery and expression of her own unique voice? And how do we define what voice means?

When I first met Jane, the whole concept of voice was entirely new to me—and it's still not always easy to define. Jane introduced me to the idea during our first lunch together and then helped me understand it more through her writing:

Voice goes two ways. It's about learning to get in touch, listen to and trust your own instincts; it's about threading instinct and experience into the fulcrum of sharp, clear expression. Born at the intersection of tentativity and certainty, it requires both vulnerability and presence.... Leaders need to find their own voices, their own best resources for being genuine in the midst of their organization, and they need to invite and to host the fullest presence of their colleagues. To have voice is to be fully present, to feel counted in, and counted on, to have something to say, and to be heard. The payoff for working in an organization in which everyone brings real voice to their work is a full measure of energy, balance, understanding, and fun.[11]

I think all leaders would like to have that kind of voice! Jane's words inspire me to work toward being "fully present" as well as to "host the fullest presence" of my colleagues—skills that demand well-developed communication skills as we experiment with discovering our voice. When I first took my seat at the leadership table—despite the fact that my master's degree is in communication—I underestimated how vital a skill having a unique voice would prove to be. Over time, I recognized that certain tools would be required in the ordinary course of everyday communication, the smaller settings that all leaders find themselves in moment to moment. My journey as a communicator began not on a platform, but in small offices and meeting rooms, over lunches and breakfasts at local restaurants, and sitting on living room couches interacting with volunteers. Before exploring the art of communicating to and teaching larger groups, we must assess whether our toolbox includes what is needed for these intimate, frequent, daily interactions.

Communicating effectively is not optional for a leader—it is absolutely essential.

Essential Tools for Everyday Communication

Communicating effectively is not optional for a leader—it is absolutely essential. Not all leaders will be required to speak in front of large groups, but all leaders are engaging in the fine art of communication all the time, in every encounter, both verbally and nonverbally. We neglect developing communication skills to our peril. Every connection with someone on our team is an opportunity for influence, vision clarification, reinforcement of values, or simply a chance to encourage, inspire, or correct. A leader's voice emerges in the accumulation of these smaller moments, and we must commit ourselves to discovering and developing that unique voice.

Developing Your Voice in Everyday Communication

One way I've learned to be intentional about developing my voice is to routinely reflect back on specific meetings or conversations. Taking time to assess my behavior in these encounters helps me to recognize whether my voice is growing stronger and more consistent day by day. I typically do this by asking myself a series of questions about how I functioned in a situation, and whether I am making progress in developing my voice. Here are some of the questions I've found helpful for assessing my voice in everyday communications:

- Did I really own my point of view in that meeting? Did I show up with a strong sense of my instincts and perspective on the issues we explored?
- Once I got into the flow of the conversation, especially if others expressed bold points of view, did I second-guess myself at every turn?
- Did I too readily assent when confronted with someone else's point of view?
- Was I congruent, or was there a difference between what I really thought and what I said? How much hiding did I do?
- What was my tone when it came to something I felt strongly about? Did my demeanor sync with the passion I felt, or did I try to protect myself by acting as though I didn't care so much?
- What was my degree of participation in the meeting? Did I monopolize the conversation, remain noticeably silent, or did I get the balance about right?
- Later in the day, did I think of all kinds of things I *wished* I would have said or communicated differently, or was I satisfied with how I showed up?

It may be helpful to occasionally ask a trusted coworker to

reflect on these questions with you. Soliciting feedback from colleagues is like holding up a mirror to see more accurately how you behave and communicate in meetings, and whether the people you work with see patterns in the degree to which your voice truly comes through. Most of us have blind spots about how we come across to others, and the huge challenge is to find ways to see ourselves more clearly and to identify where we are strong and where we need to improve.

With the frenetic pace of many of our lives, superb listening skills are quite rare and more essential than ever before.

Closely connected to developing one's voice is the need to practice some basic communication skills that are essential for all leaders. While the following discussion may seem like Interpersonal Communications 101, I am continually surprised by how often leaders—including me—need to be reminded of and refreshed on these fundamental practices.

Developing Basic Skills for Everyday Communication

When I reflect on the basic skills required of all leaders as they communicate in smaller settings, I think of four primary tools we cannot do without: attentive listening, perceptive questions, teachable moments, and talking back.

1. Attentive listening. Most of us immediately think about talking when we hear the word *communication*. But a far more essential tool is the art of active listening. In the presence of a skilled listener, we feel freed up, safe to tell our stories, and enormously valued. My friend Corinne is one of the best listeners I know. She displays a stunning capacity for giving attention to any individual she locks eyes with. When I have the privilege of sitting with Corinne, I know that for those moments, she is *fully present*, not at all distracted by anyone else who might walk by, or with her own agenda and plans for the day. For right then, I am her highest priority and she seems endlessly fascinated by whatever I have to say, no matter how trivial or mundane it may seem to me. Corinne gives others the gift of her eyes, her energy, her full engagement.

With the frenetic pace of many of our lives, superb listening skills are quite rare and more essential than ever before. When a colleague or team member stops a leader in the hallway or comes in for a one-on-one meeting, it's time to turn off the cell phones, ignore the beep of the desktop computer receiving yet another email, and offer the gift of attention. If other concerns cannot be ignored, then don't fake it—simply ask if the conversation can be rescheduled at a time you can more fully engage.

I have a mind that loves to fast-forward when someone else is speaking to me, wondering what that next thought might be, crafting my own response, and impulsively interrupting with a brilliant comment or observation. Not at all good listening! We need to learn to breathe in conversations, to remember that only a few extra moments are required to slow down our responses and give the other person room to really communicate. I have one friend who nervously completes other people's sentences before they're done speaking, as though she can't wait for the finish. This often means that both of us are saying the last few words of a sentence in unison, which is really weird and awkward. The goal is to listen in such a way that the other person feels like nothing else matters to you more in that moment than hearing and *understanding* the meaning of what is being said.

2. Perceptive questions. In addition to listening well, leaders need to ask perceptive questions. Perceptive questions are ones that move beyond the obvious and pull out the best thinking of the person talking, taking the conversation to a deeper level. Leaders are tempted, even when they engage in attentive listening, to immediately respond with an answer, a solution, or a well-crafted recommendation. We think of ourselves as *the answer person*. However, in the process of dialogue, the art of asking perceptive questions often serves a leader much better.

There is no greater model for posing superb questions than our leader, Jesus Christ. A walk through any of the four gospels yields many examples of times Jesus unnerved someone with a probing question. In Luke 10:25–37, an expert in the law stands up to test Jesus by asking, "'Teacher, what must I do to inherit eternal life?'" I think most of us would immediately respond with a pat answer, perhaps the four spiritual laws or a Scripture quote. Not Jesus. He comes right back with a question of his own: "'What is written in the Law? How do you read it?'" By urging the man to do some thinking of his own, to recall what he had already learned in the law, Jesus engages him in a far more interactive dialogue, which eventually leads to the story of the good Samaritan and even more questions to process the meaning of that illustration.

❉❉*❉*❉*❉*❉*❉*

Perceptive questions are focused on the other person, seeking to understand them or helping them to better understand themselves.

❉❉*❉*❉*❉*❉*❉*❉*

When a leader asks us a perceptive question, we are inclined to respond with a greater sense of responsibility and ownership—we recognize our own worth in coming to a solution, rather than just expecting the leader to figure it all out. That's because perceptive questions are focused on the other person, seeking to understand them or helping them to better understand themselves.

Sitting across the desk from Judson, one of the men on my first team, I knew he was stuck in a job description that no longer captivated him and no longer produced the kind of results we needed. Surely Judson knew this too. Uncertain how to nudge him off the stuck place and what to recommend as a next step, I decided to ask him a few questions: "Judson, what kind of job description would you write for yourself if the church was willing to pay you for anything you proposed? What would that job look like? How would you invest your hours every week in a way that would propel you out of bed every morning, excited to head over to church, with a sense of deep fulfillment that this is a job you were absolutely born to do?"

Judson looked at me with disbelief. He couldn't imagine anyone really caring to build a job description around his strengths,
to custom design something that would free him to focus on his
best possible contribution. I called it the Disneyland Job Description, and though I didn't promise we could pay him for whatever
he proposed, I did promise to pay close attention to his dreams and
do whatever I could to advocate for that role if we could match it
to the church's needs. My question initiated a process that resulted
in a new role for Judson, one that has continued to morph over
the years and one that I believe helped keep him in ministry for
the long haul. Judson serves with joy and he's doing what he was
created to do. A big part of his transformation began with some
perceptive questions.

Can you think of a key moment in your ministry experience
when someone asked you a perceptive question? How did that make
you feel? If you are at all like me, you felt deeply valued knowing
that the listener not only heard you, but wanted to probe deeper
and seek greater understanding. You may have marveled a bit that
someone was giving you the priceless gift of rapt attention.

When leading others, lean into the fine art of posing great
questions. This is not a sign of weakness, somehow second class
to always providing an answer. Your interactive approach will
most often lead to a more empowering relationship, and to the
kind of long-term ownership and commitment you seek from
your teammates.

3. Teachable moments. In every encounter a leader has with an
individual or group, potential hangs in the air for what I call a
teachable moment. These are spontaneous opportunities for a
leader to clarify vision or reinforce a fundamental value—to essentially say, *This is who we are*—and *this is who we are not.* Leaders
create a culture, and establishing a kind of DNA for that culture
includes how we interact with one another, how we treat those in
our community, and all the messages we want to communicate
and be known for. Occasionally, something specific happens that
triggers a strong reaction in a good leader because a core value

has been violated, and we know that unless we call attention to it, we can easily veer off course. There are also key moments when a leader observes a core value strongly upheld and reinforces that value by celebrating the victory.

Certainly parents know all about capturing teachable moments with their children. I remember a time (okay, this has happened more than once) when one of my daughters spoke especially unkind words to her sister. I brought them together, looked them in the eyes, and said, "In this family, we are kind to one another. Out there in the world, all of us will encounter people who are not always going to be kind to us. But inside this house, we will be a refuge for one another. This is the one place where you can expect to be loved and treated with care. So the tone and choice of words I just heard spoken are not acceptable, and I expect you to apologize to your sister and to take much greater care with your words to her in the future." I wish I could say I had to make that kind of speech only once, but you wouldn't believe me anyway!

Similarly, in a ministry setting, we have opportunities to look teammates in the eyes and say, "On this team, we are all about (fill in the blank)." A specific situation can serve as the best launching opportunity for one of these defining moments. For example, I recall an era when our church was growing faster than our staff and volunteer leadership could responsibly handle. While we were thrilled with all the new people coming our way, we were also overwhelmed with the task of creating a community in which attenders would feel known, appreciated, and meaningfully included in the adventure of serving.

Don't miss the opportunity to seize teachable moments when you can clarify your core values and inspire your team to get back on track.

At one of our staff meetings, Bill Hybels spoke directly and boldly about reports he was receiving from people in the congregation stating that staff members did not respond to their phone calls (this was in the days before email). Bill told us this was unacceptable. He knew that if people in the congregation felt lost in the "bigness" of the church, it could undermine everything we wanted to be about, especially one of our mantras that *People matter to God and, therefore, they must matter to us.* To drive home his point, Bill said that if he heard any report of a staff member not returning a phone call, he would personally track down that person and their job would be on the line. That certainly captured our attention! And we got the message. We recognized that not responding promptly to individuals flies in the face of *who we are* or at least *who we want to be.* We want to be known for treasuring people as individuals and honoring them with our attention.

Don't miss the opportunity to seize teachable moments when you can clarify your core values and inspire your team to get back on track.

4. Talking back. Growing up, my parents frequently told my siblings and me that we were not allowed to *talk back.* I've also spoken those very words to my own kids on occasion and, for the most part, I believe there is an appropriate lesson for children to learn about accepting—without excessive arguing—the directives of their parents. The problem is that for many adults, especially women, this pattern of submission continues beyond childhood. Added to that is the fact that while both men and women can struggle with talking back, generally in our culture men get rewarded for it and women are often put down. Many women need to develop the skill of talking back—the ability to present an alternative view, challenge the status quo, and to exert one's own unique voice. Talking back effectively does not require a leader to be strident, offensive, controlling, or hostile. Rather, a woman leader must develop her talking back muscles from an inner core of strongly held values and beliefs, and from a willingness to face her fears and even harness her anger in order to communicate with clarity, logic, and passion.

I have almost always worked with men who seem to be crystal clear on what they think and who express their points of view with strength and conviction. Their boldness conveys so much authority that it's easy to take what they say at face value and think, "Well, they must be right if they feel that strongly about it."

I would always be surprised later by instances in which that male leader admitted he was wrong! Learning that even the best leaders are not right 100 percent of the time has been a sobering reality that beckons me to wrestle more with what *I* think, with what *I* believe, and with moments when *I* must be courageous enough to talk back. This can be terrifying, and yet talking back is an absolutely essential tool in a leader's communication toolbox.

About three years ago, I found myself in a situation in which I had to talk back. We were in the midst of massive transition in our church, which included a reorganization of many departments, including the arts ministry. I was not blind to the fact that we needed to make some changes, but when church leaders revealed a new organizational structure for my department, I knew I disagreed with their decisions. In addition, I could not support the manner in which these changes would be made and how some of the individuals I had worked with for so long would be treated.

There are times when all leaders need to show up with another point of view even if that means they are in the minority.

I vividly recall one meeting in which the plan was being laid out to key staff members and how overwhelmed I felt at the thought of expressing my strong opposition. It was as though a huge tidal wave of change was already so far advanced that my little whisper of protest had no hope of being heard or respected. In that meeting, as well as in individual encounters over the next several months, I attempted to voice my concerns with honesty, passion, dignity, and objectivity. But I did not succeed. Sometimes my emotions got the better of me and my words lacked the strength of evidence and a well-developed point of view. Sometimes I caved in to the persuasive power of other voices, knowing that I could not effectively compete. At one point, I risked expressing my anger and was so frightened by the heated response that I left the room feeling even more angry and defeated.

Looking back at that era of my leadership, I regret the weakness of my talking back skills. I thought I had no power, no chance, no real hope of turning the tide and arresting the changes before it was too late. And the truth is, even if I had better skills, the outcome may have been the same. Still, I was not well prepared as a leader for the key moments when my voice needed to be stronger, wiser, a clarion call that would at least command a response of respect and the right to be fully heard.

There are times when all leaders need to show up with another point of view even if that means they are in the minority, feeling somewhat isolated and different. To return once more to the wise words of Jane Stephens:

> Real voice is the experience of speaking and *not* leaving. Of saying what we know and feeling it ring true all the way down to our shoes, and continuing to stand in them. Of feeling strong as we stand and hearing the words and meanings that come back to us as we're standing strong in our own voice.[12]

The more often we risk "standing strong in our own voice," even in small encounters with just one other person or a team, the more likely we will be able to stand strong on the bigger issues. All of this takes practice, day to day, and none of us gets really good at this skill overnight. But we really can get better.

How skilled are you at talking back? Have you found your voice in meetings or in one-on-one encounters? Do you feel capable of disagreeing? Can you challenge another point of view with inner strength and a clear articulation of your perspective? If you still need work on these talking back muscles, as I do, I encourage you to face whatever fears stand in your way. Perhaps it is the possibility you won't be liked by everyone, that you will be met with an even stronger argument, that you won't be able to persuade others.

None of these outcomes are as terrible as we fear them to be. The more we risk taking some chances, the more we will discover that the world doesn't stop spinning when we talk back, and we can actually move on.

Author and business consultant Patrick Lencioni teaches that all healthy teams know how to fight fairly, to make room for a variety of viewpoints, to disagree and still treat others well. These skills are rare, especially in Christian circles, and especially, I regret to admit, for women in those leadership circles. I want to talk back better, more often, and without so much fear. I hope you do too.

As we grow in our ability to listen attentively, to ask perceptive questions, to seize defining moments, and to talk back, we will soar in the level of influence we have with individuals and teams. We are always communicating — the real issue is how effective that communication is.

And Then I Was Asked to Teach!

From the earliest days of our church, when we met in a local movie theater, I had occasionally read Scripture in the Sunday morning service, made some introductory comments, or given announcements. I also began teaching workshops at the training conferences we conducted for other churches. Those experiences still felt far removed from actually giving a message on Sunday morning. So I was stunned when Bill called me into his office one day and asked if I would be willing to give the Mother's Day message. Up until that point, we had not had any women teachers on a regular basis at our church. In fact, the extremely short list of non-male communicators up to that point included Jill Briscoe and the sister of former president Jimmy Carter.

My mind raced with a million hesitations as I tried to figure out how to respond. I have extremely high standards for teaching because I have always been surrounded by excellent communicators. I didn't yet know if God had entrusted me with the gift of teaching and, if so, whether I could develop that gift to the level required and expected at my church. I also knew I was no expert on mothering, having been a parent for just four years. Would more seasoned moms be willing to listen to this rookie? And how would the congregation respond to a woman teaching? Was our church even ready for this step?

Despite these hesitations, a quiet voice inside encouraged me to take the risk and accept the challenge. Thus began my journey as a woman teacher, one that eventually led to my inclusion on our staff as a teaching pastor.

Discovering that I was entrusted with the gift of teaching should not have come as such a shock to me. I now see that God was preparing me all along to employ this gift, tracing back to the excellent training I received when competing on our high school speech team. Bill had wisely introduced me to the congregation slowly over a long period of time through the smaller opportunities for communication. People in the church already felt they knew me and, I believe, trusted me as a person and as a Christ-follower.

Yet, as for any other potential teacher, a time of experimentation began to reveal whether or not my teaching gift would be effective. The most obvious test for whether someone has a teaching gift transpires when the communicator can see how listeners respond. Are people engaged when you speak? Do they grasp and then act on the truths being conveyed? And, perhaps most obvious, do they show up when you teach again and seem to want more?

I recognize that many Christians still disagree with the idea that a woman preaching is acceptable according to Scripture and tradition (my own mother prefers to tell people I am a *teacher*, not a *preacher*). When I began to teach, there were some in the congregation who wrestled with their own beliefs on the issue, who met with our elders, and in some cases, who ended up leaving the church to look for a place where their views were supported. Bill and the elders protected me from most of these communications, but I knew there was some controversy over my presence in the pulpit.

And so on that bright morning in May, I walked onstage with shaking knees (my friends on the production team who sat in the front row let me know they could see the vibrations through my pant legs) and an even shakier voice. I had to engage in all kinds of self-talk just to persevere through those early experiences of teaching, including telling myself that all those people listening were *for me*, not against me, that a huge majority of people are terrified of public speaking, that God through his Holy Spirit had given me a message to convey and would empower me, and that all I could be expected to do was to give my very best. I recognized that part of my challenge lay in not comparing myself to other teachers, knowing that over the years I had developed extremely high standards based on the quality of communicators from whom I had been privileged to learn.

> *I had to learn what it meant to be fully myself, comfortable in my own skin, and willing to express myself authentically as a woman of faith.*

My role models for superb teaching in the church have almost all been men: Bill Hybels, John Ortberg, Andy Stanley, Erwin McManus, Donald Miller, Harvey Carey, Wayne Cordeiro. How could I find my own voice and not cave in to copying the men I so deeply respected? Surely, I needed to learn from these role models without somehow trying to clone myself to be just like them, right? Once again, I had to learn what it meant to be fully myself, comfortable in my own skin, and willing to express myself authentically as a woman of faith.

Just like anyone entrusted with the gift of teaching, I realize that I can and should get better—through experience, listening to excellent communicators, receiving feedback from coaches and perceptive listeners, and seizing any opportunities for further training. But my biggest challenge as a teacher centers on carving out my unique voice as I learn what it means to listen to my own life and to the whispers of God.

Listening to My Life

The best communicators I know practice the art of paying attention to their lives, to all the everyday moments and experiences that serve to teach us, remind us of God's holy presence, and provide the basis for the telling of stories that connect to and identify with others. For years, I have been struck by the challenge of author and pastor Frederick Buechner to pay attention, including these words from his book, *Now and Then*:

> Taking your children to school and kissing your wife goodbye. Eating lunch with a friend. Trying to do a decent day's work. Hearing the rain patter against the window. There is no event so commonplace but that God is present within it, always hiddenly, always leaving you room to recognize him or not to recognize him, but all the more fascinatingly because of all that, all the more compellingly and hauntingly.... If I were called upon to state in a few words the essence of everything I was trying to say both as a novelist and as a preacher, it would be something like this: Listen to your life. See it for the fathomless mystery that it is. In the boredom and pain of it no less than in the excitement and gladness: touch, taste, smell your way to the holy and hidden heart of it because in the last analysis all moments are key moments, and life itself is grace.[13]

Unless I listen to my life, I have no hope of developing my own authentic and unique voice. It is out of the stuff of the seemingly ordinary, everyday moments I encounter—as a daughter, friend, wife, mother, neighbor, worker, and child of God—that I hear the whispers of the Spirit, recognize the common temptations and trials of simply being human, and make connections that God can use to breathe life and understanding into the lives of others.

Communication is all about connection. We have all listened to messages from people who might be scary-smart, full of fascinating and not-so-fascinating information, and yet who fail to build any kind of bridge that draws us in and identifies with our own journey. Of course, this speaks to the remarkable power of story. Messages that connect are most often built on stories told with honesty, skill, warmth, and sometimes humor. Stories that cause the listener to say, "Yes, I get it, and I have been in a similar place."

When I meet someone from our church for the first time, they often comment on one of my messages—and it is almost always the stories they remember. One time I was teaching about patience and told a story about my impatience when Johanna, my younger daughter, kept misplacing her retainer. When we returned from church one Saturday evening, Jo came up to me with fear in her big blue eyes and let me know that she had lost the retainer yet again. She thought she had probably dropped it earlier that day when we got into the car to come home from church. *Oh, great.* The parking lot at our church is massive—nearly four thousand spaces—and it was already dusk. It was completely absurd to think we even had a shot at finding this tiny piece of expensive orthodontic plastic.

If you teach and preach, do not try to be someone you are not.

With tremendous irritation in my voice, I told Johanna to get in the car and we would make the trip back to church—which was likely to prove both futile and ridiculous. Later, Johanna told me she was quietly praying all the way to the parking lot that we would somehow find the retainer. (My daughter is much more spiritual than I am—she was praying while I was fuming!)

Most of the cars were gone by the time we arrived, and somehow I did remember roughly where we had parked, which was highly unusual for me. Imagine my absolute shock when I saw something glistening on the concrete in the fading sunlight, drove up, opened the car door, and there it was. The miracle of the found retainer. Johanna just grinned and then told me about her prayer. Humbled by my daughter's faith and the obvious lack of my own, I handed the retainer back to her and we headed home.

A few years later, people still remember the retainer story. They may not recall much else I taught in that message on patience, but they do remember every detail of our little miracle. Whenever we open up our lives and share stories, as long as they are appropriate and we are given permission by the other characters in the story to share, the listeners feel a connection to us. I am learning that people in our congregation—even those I have never met—feel like they know me and my family simply because of the stories I've told about the ordinary events of our lives.

As a woman communicator, it is hugely significant for me to listen to my life—from my female perspective—and to share the stories that are unique to me. I will not be telling stories about racing sailboats like Bill Hybels, driving trucks like Mike Breaux, surfing like John Ortberg, or leading people to Christ on airplanes like my friend Lee Strobel. I will be telling my own stories that take place in my Pilates class, at my book club, in gymnasiums watching my daughter play basketball, in restaurants with my husband.

As I listen to my life and tell my stories, a voice emerges. It is my voice, and it connects to people in ways the voices of others cannot. While I may not think the everyday moments of my life are worth sharing, the truth is that my listeners are a whole lot more like me than I know. I actually have great potential for connecting simply because my life is rather ordinary, and yet spectacular at the same time when I see it in the light of God's presence and power. Educator and author Parker Palmer says a good teacher must stand in the vulnerable overlap of public and private life, "dealing with the thunderous flow of traffic at an intersection where 'weaving a web of connectedness' feels more like crossing the freeway on foot."[14] We must have the courage to stand in that intersection and allow our lives to be opened up and shared.

If you teach and preach, do not try to be someone you are not. Do not mimic the style, voice, and stories of others in an effort to be accepted. Trust that God has given you a voice that needs to be heard and stories that will connect if you tell them with a spirit of openness, discovery, and reflection on eternal truth. We are all of us telling the greatest story of all, the story of redemption through the person of Jesus Christ. As we communicate the truths of Scripture, we apply that truth through the prism of our own experience, and the Holy Spirit does transforming work in the hearts and minds of those who listen. Pay attention to every possible moment in your everyday experiences so you can be a woman who examines her soul and who is used by God to breathe life into others.

Listening to God

I often bristle when I hear people express doubt that God still works amazing miracles today, because one of the most astounding examples of supernatural power I know takes place whenever a Christ-follower gets quiet and hears the still, small voice of our Creator. When I agree to speak at our church or at a conference, it is most essential that I carve out time and room to hear that still, small voice, and to discern by the power of the Spirit what God would have me communicate. Most often, my work begins with a study of Scripture, with whatever truth I am asked to explore and dig into. As we listen, God uses his Word, along with the experiences of our daily lives, to guide and shape what needs to be shared with our audience. And the very fact that God still speaks today to anyone willing to pay attention, whether we are driving a car, taking a shower, walking in our neighborhood, or sitting in a coffee shop, truly astounds me. I call that a miracle.

In the busyness of everyday life, any leader called to communicate must be devoted to the discipline of solitude. We can't hear God's voice coming through the din of a day if it is entirely filled with noise, hurry, distractions, and interruptions. I also believe that my time of message and teaching preparation deserves the best hours of my day, which, in my case, is the morning. Under the tutelage of other leaders, I have learned to zealously protect as many mornings as I can from other meetings and obligations. Most mornings, I can be found at the local Panera Bread or Caribou Coffee, sitting with my cup of tea and my laptop. In this space of

In the busyness of everyday life, any leader called to communicate must be devoted to the discipline of solitude.

solitude, I try to make room for the Holy Spirit to penetrate my thoughts, to make my study clear, to help me know how to craft and illustrate a message.

In writing his letter to the church at Corinth, the apostle Paul reveals the mystery of how God communicates through his people: "This is what we speak, not in words taught us by human wisdom but in words taught by the Spirit, explaining spiritual realities with Spirit-taught words" (1 Cor. 2:13). I will never get over the wonder that God has gifted men and women to be his voice to a community, to articulate the timeless truths of Scripture and apply them to our current realities with relevance and authenticity. If I had to lean on human wisdom without the anointing power of the Spirit and the words he guides me to speak, I would be just another speaker, not a messenger from God. When I get alone and quiet, I try to remember the holiness of the task, without getting overwhelmed. We must remember that God loves our churches more than we do, and he wants the entire service and the message time to impact his people as well as connect with those not yet committed to him.

We assume the responsibility to listen for guidance, to grow in our craft, to diligently study and prepare, and to deliver our messages with passion and a freed-up spirit. Then we entrust the outcome to the only One who can truly transform lives. If you regularly prepare messages for a team or congregation, ask yourself if you are making enough room to listen to God. As you pay attention to his voice, you will be shown the way to finding your own voice.

I have now been teaching regularly for about thirteen years. At times I have been called upon to bring a word of encouragement, to inspire people to seize the day and to live their best possible life. In other messages, I have been asked to stretch the minds of the congregation, to introduce truths that require us to wrestle deeply as we examine Scripture and apply it to our everyday experience. I have taught from the Old Testament and the New, always getting far more out of my study and preparation than those who listen likely do. One aspect of my role as a communicator in the church emerged slowly over time and has surprised me and given me pause. This is the capacity Jane Stephens calls "the power of benediction" or giving a blessing. I saw what a vital role benediction and blessing play most vividly the weekend after the horrific events of September 11, 2001.

On the afternoon of the tragic Tuesday when the United States was reeling from the terrorist attacks on the World Trade Center, our leadership team huddled in Bill's office. We recognized, like church leaders all over the country, that whatever we had planned for the following Sunday would need to be tossed out. We needed to prayerfully prepare a whole new service in order to minister to the pain, confusion, anxiety, and extreme loss our community was experiencing.

In addition to the obvious decisions about the content of those key services, we also asked the *who* question—who from our pastoral and arts teams needed to be visible and present for our congregation at this critical juncture? The first and obvious answer was our senior pastor; Bill would bring the primary message that day. But almost as quickly, the team looked at me and asked if I would be willing to lead a time of prayer and spiritual direction. The consensus was that the congregation needed to hear my voice as well.

Our church is not the only one that was full to overflowing that September weekend. Cars were parked blocks away when our parking lot filled up, and all three of our services were full to capacity with overflow. When tragedy struck, even those on the fringe of our community and many who hadn't crossed the threshold of a church in years showed up because life felt shaky, and the only place many could think to turn was to God and to faith. There was a desperate longing for hope and community, and wisdom fueled by an acute awareness that nothing would ever be quite the same again, that our very foundations as a country were rocked and far more fragile than we had ever known before. And so we came to church, searching for some way to make sense of it all or at least to find a shred of comfort by being together and offering up our questions and our prayers.

As I ministered that morning, expressing my own horror, guiding the congregation into the presence of the sovereign God, not hiding my own confusion and pain, I knew I was right where I was supposed to be. I took a deep breath, described with a genuine heart the state I was in and the condition I knew they were in, read the timeless words of truth from the Psalms to ground us with an eternal perspective, and prayed an authentic prayer with a voice that cried out to God for help and refuge. These moments were needful, just as the song of comfort that followed and the message from Bill. God used my voice as a vital part of our team and as a key member of our church family.

At various times, some members of the congregation have expressed to me that they see me as the "mom" of our church. I admit to feeling uncertain about that label. But to be a mother is a noble calling, and our God is described in Scripture as both father and mother to his children. Other folks have said, "Nancy, you're the *heart* of our church," and describe other leaders as the *head*. While I struggle with the stereotype that women leaders are more expressive with their emotions and feelings, I also recognize the power of being

Without your voice, your community will not shine as brightly or be as healthy as it can be.

a force of comfort, a conduit of vulnerability, and a voice for the free expression of feelings and needs—including the need to be reassured and blessed. When I offer a benediction to our congregation, when I look them in the eyes and remind them of the vast depth of God's love for them, that he is absolutely *crazy about them*, and when I affirm their worth, I stand in awe of that holy privilege. I am increasingly okay with being a kind of mother in our community because, after all, that is a huge part of who I am and who God has called me to be.

I am still finding, forming, and learning to express my voice. The church desperately needs the voices of more women leaders, both in small settings when we clarify vision and inspire teams, and in larger gatherings when we teach workshops or give the Sunday morning message. In whatever arena you find yourself communicating, devote yourself to discovering your own unique voice and then allow your voice to be heard. We need you to be real, to tell your stories, to bless us with your perspective, to call us higher, to comfort and challenge, to identify and connect, to reveal and inspire and envision and ennoble. Without your voice, your community will not shine as brightly or be as healthy as it can be. Please listen to your life, listen to your God, and then speak the words that reveal the unique communicator God made you to be.

A Quick Note Before You Read Chapter 7

We are about to take a detour, one that may feel like an abrupt departure from the journey we've been on up to this point. But here's why I think it's important. When I began to write this book, I imagined that readers would include both men and women. All of my teaching over the years has been directed to both genders, and that approach is what comes most naturally to me. However, to my surprise, the more I dug into each chapter, the more I found myself focusing primarily on the issues and needs unique to women in leadership. As a result, each chapter turned out to be much more personal and focused on women than I imagined at the start. This change presented me with a dilemma—how could I still find a way to direct bold and clear requests to male leaders in the church if they weren't my primary readers?

And so I chose to write chapter 7, which addresses male pastors and church leaders directly. Of course, many of these leaders won't know about the chapter unless someone alerts them. I considered asking the publisher to perforate the pages so you could tear them out and hand them to the key male leaders in your community. We didn't go that far, but you get the idea. It would be wonderful if men would read or at least skim through the entire book to gain some understanding on the bigger picture and challenges faced by women leaders. But in case that does not happen, please encourage the men you know to read chapter 7. My hope is that this letter will open up some doors for dialogue and progress. And by the way, you should read it too.

SEVEN

AN OPEN LETTER TO MALE PASTORS AND CHURCH LEADERS

Dear Pastor or Church Leader,

I imagine that a woman handed you this book and said, "I won't ask you to read the whole thing, but would you be willing to read chapter 7? It was written for you." So in spite of the fact that you have piles of other things to read and may be hesitant to even pick up a book like this one, you have at least hung with me to this sentence. And I thank you. It is a testimony to your willingness to explore the subject of women in church leadership that you carved out these few minutes. I value your time, and I'll do my best to get right to the point.

I write on behalf of women from all over this planet who love Jesus Christ and who have been entrusted with the gifts of leadership and teaching. I write on behalf of the women leaders in your church—those you know and those who have not yet emerged or come out of hiding. What I have to say is based not only on my own experience but also on countless conversations with women who long to play a significant role in the church, women who are already leading or who linger on the sidelines, wondering if there is a place for them. Although I am just one voice, I come to you with confidence that I can speak authentically for many women who want to contribute their leadership and teaching gifts to the church.

Maybe you are already on the front lines of providing meaningful opportunities and significant support for women leaders and teachers. If that is the case, my words will simply underscore much of what you are already doing and perhaps give you some additional thoughts on which to reflect. Or maybe you would admit to having concerns and reservations about the role of women in church leadership. If so, I ask only that you read with an open mind and spirit.

Once you have chosen a point of view on women in leadership, I encourage you to hold that perspective with a spirit of humility and continued openness. Craig Blomberg, one of the complementarian contributors to the book *Two Views on Women in Ministry*, exhorts us with these words:

> All of us who speak and write on gender roles would do well to begin and end every address with the caveats, "I could be wrong" and, "I respect the right of fellow evangelicals and evangelical churches to come to different conclusions, and I will cooperate with them rather than combat them for the larger cause of Christ and his kingdom, which so desperately needs such unity."[15]

May all of us display such a gracious and respectful spirit on this issue which can so easily degenerate into divisiveness and rancor. For the sake of the kingdom, we must be exceedingly careful with our words and our attitudes.

I want to begin by exploring *what* I am challenging you to do, with an attempt to be highly specific with a call to action. I will then follow up with a description of *why* this matters so much for your congregation, your community, your own leadership and staff, and for the next generation.

What I Am Challenging You to Do

When it comes to specific action steps, I urge you to take up a threefold challenge: to engage in diligent study on the issue of women in leadership in the church, to make this a front-burner issue, and to be the strongest advocate you can be for women with leadership and teaching gifts.

Engage in Diligent Study

All of us hold tightly to a picture of what we think the right and biblical role for women in the church should be. Our picture is formed largely from our backgrounds, our education, the traditions of whatever churches or denominations we have participated in, and our personal experiences of women in leadership. However helpful these influences may be, they are incomplete on their own. Unfortunately, too many leaders have yet to engage in their own personal study and are not equipped to

Consider putting together a small team of leaders at your church, including some or all of your elders, to engage in an honest and penetrating study together.

intelligently and clearly articulate the basis for their position. This weakness includes both those who lean toward a complementarian view (ministry roles differentiated by gender) as well as those who hold to an egalitarian view (equal ministry opportunities for both genders). You are probably an exception, but the majority of leaders I encounter—men and women—haven't really done the homework required to work through the difficult biblical passages. As a result, they cannot give a reasonable and thorough response to their congregations or to others when asked probing questions. They lean into half-baked or trite answers that fail to satisfy and lack the depth required of such a profoundly significant issue.

So I ask you, how diligently have you studied? Have you read through books that present a variety of viewpoints? Have you wrestled honestly with the context and background of all the difficult biblical passages? Are you able to defend your position soundly, or do you default to the way things have always been in your church or denomination?

In appendix 1 (page 181), I list several books that could be a starting place for your study. I encourage you to make the time for this kind of study, and to approach your exploration with as open a mind as possible, as though you are starting from ground zero, setting aside preconceptions and previous understandings. Better yet, consider putting together a small team of leaders at your church, including some or all of your elders, to engage in an honest and penetrating study together.

In the early years of our church, that's precisely what our elders did. Granted, as a nondenominational church we certainly had the freedom to start with a blank sheet of paper and wrestle with the issue until we gained consensus. For several months, our elders dug in, studied, and dialogued about what they were learning. No matter how they would have landed at the end of the day, I will be forever grateful for their diligence. They earned the respect of our congregation, even the respect of those who did not agree with the position paper that resulted (included on page 201 of appendix 3). No one could say they glossed over the issue.

I ask you to place the issue of women in leadership in the top tier of your concerns.

Pastors and church leaders, please commit to engaging in your own diligent study. I acknowledge that reading some of the books and commentaries can make a person feel even more confused, because the issue is so complex and those who hold firmly to either view are quite convincing as they present their arguments. But we must be willing to handle the dissonance and persevere through the work—and we must make it a priority.

Make This a Front-Burner Issue

My experience on the senior leadership team at a growing church gave me a front row seat to the variety of issues church leaders deal with on a regular basis, and I understand how those many issues compete for primary attention. We knew we could not and should not place too many concerns on the front burner, and so we needed to prayerfully choose the issues that would be most important in the life of our church during a given season. Of course, every leader on the team had strong opinions about what those front-burner issues should be, and fiercely defended them as we engaged in animated and passionate discussions. Those were healthy discussions, and I thoroughly enjoyed the sometimes-heated exchanges because they indicated how much we all really cared.

My guess is that you have at least a dozen *really big deals* at your church right now, issues that shout for your atten-

> *"It will increasingly damage the credibility of the gospel if the church becomes the one place in society where women and men cannot serve together as equal co-bearers of the image of God."*

tion and are truly critical to the health, vitality, and effectiveness of your community. Nevertheless, I ask you to place the issue of women in leadership in the top tier of your concerns. Women in leadership is one of those issues—along with becoming more racially diverse and multicultural—that we can too easily put aside, hesitate for months to really look at, and secretly hope to overlook because we know how messy and complex the work will be. Rarely do we view such issues as urgent in light of all the other apparent emergencies waving their red flags.

And yet, this issue is far more urgent than what may appear on the surface, and the stakes for getting it right are extremely high. In a recent conversation, author and senior pastor John Ortberg stated, "It will increasingly damage the credibility of the gospel if the church becomes the one place in society where women and men cannot serve together as equal co-bearers of the image of God." Whether or not you currently agree with that assertion, the issue begs for all church leaders to actively engage in the quest for intelligent, Spirit-led guidance on the fundamental principles involved. We simply must not be apathetic about such a vital issue.

One way to increase the urgency level is to intentionally invest some time listening to the women in your congregation. Why not invite a few women with leadership gifts, either individually or in a small group, to go to lunch with you or meet in your office? It takes a lot of guts to open up these issues with the people most affected by your decisions. But if you are willing to ask some key questions and genuinely listen, women leaders will feel like they really do matter enough for someone at your level to actually inquire and to seek a fuller understanding.

If you are willing to take this courageous step, here are a few questions you might consider asking the women you meet with:

- What kinds of opportunities have you been given to lead in our church? Do those opportunities line up with your interests and passions?
- When it comes to expressing your point of view and contributing to strategic decisions, how safe do you feel on teams with men in our church?
- Describe your experience of our church culture when it comes to women leading and teaching.
- What kinds of limitations have you sensed at our church for the use of your gifts?
- Have we clearly articulated our position on women in leadership in a way that makes sense to you?
- Do the male teachers and communicators here ever say things that are less inclusive than they should be, or sometimes hurtful even if we don't intend for them to be so?
- What else is important for me to know?

If you ask these questions, your next job is to be quiet and listen to the responses. Resist the temptation to get defensive or engage in an argument. Your mission is to uncover the experience of these women so you can be empathetic and accurately assess the state of your current reality. I guarantee that if you are willing to dialogue with the women in your church, your own sense of urgency about the issue of their role will increase. Let them come out of hiding and talk openly with you; you may be surprised and sobered by what you hear, and in some cases, encouraged. But you won't really know if you never ask. Once you have done the job of listening, you will be far more likely to show up as an advocate for women leaders in whatever ways you can.

Be the Strongest Advocate You Can Be for Women with Leadership and Teaching Gifts

I don't know where your diligent study and dialogue with women leaders will land you in terms of your church's position on the issue. But wherever you land, there is more than likely lots of room for you to either open doors for women to contribute in influential roles, or to passively allow things to continue on in the way they've always been. Even if your church decides against allowing women to be pastors or elders, there is still a lot of room for them to lead in vital areas in your church — and I don't mean exclusively in children's or women's ministries.

If you were to visit your church as someone who had never been there before, how many women would you see in meaningful roles? Are there women who usher, women who read Scripture from the platform, women who contribute in meaningful ways to the worship and arts experience, women who guide the congregation in prayer or who give significant announcements? Think through the entire week in the life of your church — are there roles open to women in terms of discipleship training, strategic leadership in the various missions of your church, opportunities for them in a variety of ministries to have a strong voice and build effective teams?

The truth is that, as a male leader, you hold the keys to most of the pivotal roles in your church, to the recruiting and development of core volunteers, and also to how staff positions are filled. How many of these roles are open equally to men and to women? Are there more of these assignments for which you could intentionally seek qualified women candidates? In addition, take a look at the next generation of emerging women in your church and objectively ask yourself whether anyone is focused on developing their potential for the future. Will young women in your community perceive there are places where they could fully express their gifts, or are they far more likely to steer themselves toward the corporate or academic world?

Another essential way for you to be an advocate is in your public communications. If you are a teacher at your church, examine the content of your announcements, messages, and especially your personal illustrations. How often do you uphold the dignity and worth of women? Do you use a gender-accurate translation of the Bible? What kinds of stories do you tell about women, and how often do you portray them with stereotypes or subtle humor that could be hurtful and dismissive? If you are married to a full-time homemaker, be careful not to assume that this is the experience of most of the women listening to you, or to uphold your wife's choices as superior to the choices of women who work outside the home (many of whom would say they truly have no choice). Ask a woman in your church who works in the corporate world to periodically give you feedback on your teaching and how it comes across to her. Push her to be honest with you, and then learn from her responses. Listening to male teachers in my own church and at conferences, I have experienced many "ouches" in the illustrations they've used, and I am quite sure the speakers were oblivious to the insults or wounds they inflicted. Pay close attention to your words in every setting, but especially in the pulpit, because your words and your

Women leaders offer a perspective, a voice, an entire world of experience that is essential for both men and women in the congregation to experience.

perspectives matter more than you know as you influence the hearts and minds of men and women, boys and girls.

I realize that I am asking for a lot in calling you to diligent study, to making this a front-burner issue, and to being a powerful advocate for women. All of this will cost you time and most likely even draw criticism from some of your attenders. Chances are some people could get mad enough to leave your church and you might be characterized in ways that make you uncomfortable. So the logical question we all ask when assessing cost is, "Why?" Is this course of action really worth the trouble? Let me attempt to answer the "why" question.

Why This Matters So Much

Four groups of people leap to mind when I think about why you should fully engage in this issue and be a force for change. Freeing women to lead and to teach with greater influence and authority in your church is hugely significant for the sake of your congregation, your local community, yourself and your staff, and your daughters and other emerging young women.

For the Sake of Your Congregation

A local church that limits itself primarily to the leadership and communication gifts of men misses out on many fronts. Women leaders offer a perspective, a voice, an entire world of experience that is essential for *both men and women* in the congregation to experience. Most churches have a higher percentage of women than men. And every church would have to close its doors tomorrow were it not for the women who contribute all week long to ongoing ministries. When we limit the opportunities for all of us to hear from women, to benefit from their stories, to be guided by their wisdom, to build into teams, to uncover gifts, to lend us their creativity, to contribute their strategic thinking as well as their tremendous capacity for listening and their track record for emotional and relational intelligence—well, we miss a truckload of benefits. Why would we want to do that? A congregation can only be stronger when its women are empowered as much as possible.

I am sobered when I think of women I know who, having given up on making an impact in church, are contributing their world-class gifts in other arenas—business, nonprofits, academia, etc. This ought not to be so. Far too many women have observed the reality of not having a meaningful place for ministry expression, and yet are empowered to strategize, lead, create, manage, and teach in other environments. Their professional or volunteer experience during the week contrasts starkly with their limited opportunities at church on the weekends. Meanwhile, most church teams are always on the lookout for qualified leaders to make a difference in every ministry arena. Ignoring the potential contribution of an entire gender, especially in the realm of leadership, is an enormous loss for the kingdom.

When it comes to teaching, your church also needs the contribution of women more than most male leaders recognize. I once thought the people in the church who needed most to hear from and be led by women were other women, but now I see it differently. Men need women just as much for the full formation of their souls. Recently, I was standing in line in the busy food court at O'Hare Airport, getting a salad to take on a long flight since the airlines no longer feed us. A man I did not recognize introduced himself to me as a member of our church. After we chatted for a few minutes, he paused and looked me right in the eyes and said, "I would be remiss if I didn't thank you for a brief conversation we had a year ago after you taught a Sunday morning message. You probably don't remember, but you had a major impact on me that day."

> *Men need the blessing and benediction and guidance from women leaders as much as they need these gifts from other men.*

I felt bad about not being able to recall the conversation and apologized.

He continued. "I was feeling unsure about the moment when I will meet God in heaven and be accountable for my life. I knew I was saved, but I was struggling with self-doubt and regrets. Our conversation redirected me that day. You made an enormous difference."

The clerk behind the counter let the man know his smoothie was ready. Before the man left, I saw the tears in his eyes. Something very powerful had happened as a result of our conversation over a year ago, and this man was expressing simple gratitude to one of his pastors.

More often than I can count, men have told me how much they have appreciated hearing my perspective as a teacher, or receiving kind words as I baptized them, or being challenged as a husband or father through hearing from a woman. Men need the blessing and benediction and guidance from women leaders as much as they need these gifts from other men. Just as our God is described in Scripture with words that define masculine traits, there are also times when the divine character is portrayed as distinctly feminine, even maternal (Isa. 66:13; Matt. 23:37; Ps. 91:4; Ps. 131:2). We all need both the fathering and mothering of God, and our congregations receive this wondrous gift through the voices and leadership of both men and women.

Pastors and leaders, every risk you take to free women to lead and to speak has the potential to more fully form and minister to the individuals in your church. Will you make a way for that to happen? I guarantee that over time, your church will be far healthier, more robust and balanced, filled with people who are more like Jesus because they have been so well led and well taught by men and women surrendered to God.

For the Sake of the Non-Churched in Your Community

Along with other perceptions people in your local community hold about your church, they most likely also wonder about the role of women and your view of women in leadership. This issue is one of the hot button concerns cited by pastor and author Dan Kimball as he dialogues with young people and uncovers the primary barriers that keep them from walking into a church and, more importantly, from pursuing the Christian faith. In his excellent and provocative book *They Like Jesus but Not the Church*, Dan writes, "As people outside of the church look at us, many think of us as a boys' club, concluding that the church teaches that females are not as valued and respected as men are. This conclusion keeps many people away who might otherwise trust the church enough to enter into community with us."[16]

When people far from God look at politics, the corporate arena, academic institutions, and the entertainment business, they see women of strength and skill exerting greater and greater influence. The entire subculture of the church appears outdated and out of touch with what many of these folks believe to be true about the potential, skills, and necessary opportunities for women. Would unchurched visitors feel as though they have entered a time warp attending your services, examining your leadership rosters and scratching their heads at the absence of strong women leaders?

What are we communicating to our communities about the worth and place of women, and in particular, what are we communicating to the next generation, who are passionate proponents of equal opportunity for all, regardless of skin color, socioeconomic background, and gender? Even if your church lands in a place that is fairly conservative about women in certain leadership roles, there are still significant ways in which you can uphold the worth of women and create as much room as possible for them to have influence. If we hope to be perceived as communities that are open to and in pursuit of the participation of those in the next generation, we must pay attention to the issue of women in leadership. Otherwise, many of them will simply write us off and stay away.

For Your Sake and the Sake of Your Staff

Many men in leadership already know the contribution women leaders can make, but others have not yet taken the step of inviting women to the table. Perhaps you are accustomed to meeting regularly with a group of guys, not having to worry about including women in your relationships and your decision making. That feels comfortable and—if you are willing to admit this thought—*the way it should be.* If you have no women peers in ministry, I believe you are missing several significant ways in which your own leadership could be enriched and enhanced. Effective women leaders can bring to your circle their perspective, their instincts, their creativity, their communication skills, and their instincts for emotional intelligence. Obviously, many male leaders also display these traits, but women in the circle will add a dimension to your team that more fully represents your congregation, your community, and the full image of God. Your team will be healthier and, I contend, more effective.

In her book *See Jane Lead*, Dr. Lois P. Frankel argues that women excel in the traits most commonly listed as reflecting successful leadership, including the abilities to:

- Create a vision, align people behind it, and develop a plan for executing it.
- Communicate in a way that inspires trust and confidence.
- Motivate followers to sustain the effort required to meet organizational goals.
- Build teams that understand and value interdependence and synergy.
- Exhibit emotional intelligence.
- Take risks that benefit the organization.
- Develop a strong network that supports goal attainment and professional success.[17]

Dr. Frankel states that "a close look at the list reveals that these behaviors are identical to the ones women routinely exhibit given their own socialization as nurturers, accommodators and caretakers.... Women's survival has always depended on exhibiting the very behaviors desperately needed in society today."[18]

Sitting in your church on Sunday mornings are some remarkable women, women who effectively lead in other arenas all week long, women who could be making an enormous difference in the life and direction and culture of your church. Some of the huge challenges your church currently faces require the input of these women leaders, but most of them will not come forward or offer their service if they assume they will not be welcome. Depending on what they observe at your church, they may decide it is best to hang back and linger in the shadows.

If you have already invited women leaders to the table, you know that they can also contribute immeasurably to the joy, vitality, and emotional health of your staff and volunteer teams. Most of the male leaders I know around the world who have taken this risk will admit that some of their strongest leaders are women, and that these women have provided exceedingly wise counsel at key junctures in their own (the leaders') lives and in the lives of their churches. Whether it is a result of genetics or of how they learn to adapt to the culture, women generally—not always—have excellent skills at reading a room, leaning into their instincts when it comes to human behavior, and building a team based on truth telling and mutual support. You need their presence more than you know.

Yes, there are potential risks connected to inviting women to your inner circle, including the fear of putting yourself and other male leaders in a place of temptation, crossing appropriate boundaries, getting too close to these women emotionally or physically. Men and women who serve together in church have fallen to sexual sin, whether or not the women have played a leadership role. Rather than running from the potential for trouble, I urge you to build a culture in which you talk openly about how you will treat one another, what to do if an unhealthy attraction for someone on the team emerges, how to walk with the Spirit, and how to invest in accountable relationships with those who will ask you the tough questions and help you to remain pure. This *can* be done, and the price is more than worth it.

The first time a woman sits at your leadership table or teaches from the pulpit at your church may be a little awkward. But you can prepare the team and your congregation well in advance for such a transition if you are intentional and wise. When you add a woman to your leadership team or elder board for the first time, go ahead and acknowledge the elephant in the room for everyone—there is no sense pretending that something new and different isn't happening—and allow the team to exhale and maybe even be light-hearted about it.

As for the pulpit, introduce a woman teacher slowly over time, first with shorter opportunities to give announcements, lead a guided prayer, or make some introductory comments. Let the congregation get used to the idea of this new communicator, and hopefully make a strong connection with her. Before you even get that far, be as certain as you possibly can be that you have chosen this new team member or woman teacher with tremendous care. Then place the weight of your strong support behind her in every way you can because the staff team and congregation will take their signal from you. Let everyone know, at every opportunity you can seize, that you are an advocate for this woman leader or teacher, that you have great confidence in her, and that you expect everyone to treat her with respect.

The decisions you make about women in leadership will have a ripple effect for generations to come.

I know this sounds like a lot of work with many attendant risks. Those who invite strong women to join their teams and communicate to their congregations will one day look back and be unable to imagine what life was like before women played a key role. Be the one bold enough to take these steps—for your own sake and for the sake of your church.

For the Sake of Your Daughters and the Next Generation

Okay, maybe you don't have daughters. Yet, in a sense, you do, because you are a leader in the lives of young women growing up in your church and in your community. The decisions you make about women in leadership, the extent to which you either become a force for change and a conduit for them to contribute, will have a ripple effect for generations to come. Young girls will either grow up believing there is a place for them in the life of their church, or figure out quickly that those doors are closed.

A few years ago the pastor of a church in California told me about his own journey with the issue of women in leadership. Raised in the Midwest, he grew up in a church and a denomination that was quite conservative in their position. He never saw a woman play a significant role up front in church or on a strategic leadership team. He thought that was normal and biblical and right—until he had daughters.

Then, my pastor friend told me, he started to question his background and his beliefs, especially as both his girls grew up displaying undeniable gifts of leadership and communication skills. What would he tell them about their potential in the local church, and even in the church he was leading? All of this messed with his mind, until he was willing to do the diligent study and launch a path toward slow change in a denomination that appeared closed to altering their traditional views.

The next generation of women desperately needs male leaders who will be a courageous force for transformation. Most of the power in the church around the world currently resides in the hands of men. Unless and until some are willing to revisit assumptions and rattle some cages, nothing will fundamentally change; and more and more young women devoted to Jesus Christ will simply dabble in the church, or leave, while choosing to invest their skills, instincts, and passion in the corporate world or other arenas. We will lose their potential power for the kingdom.

As I close this letter, I sit in the exquisite lobby of one of the finest hotels in the United States, stealing just a couple hours from our family vacation to meet a deadline (they're still asleep anyway). We are staying across the street in a borrowed cottage, occasionally wandering outside the gates of this hotel's magnificent pool and craning our necks to see if anyone famous is putting on their suntan lotion, because we have seen photos of this place in *People* magazine. A pastor friend told me it would be okay to take my laptop along and write in the hotel lobby, but as I sit here, I'm not too sure. The enormous displays of fresh flowers, the glistening hardwood tables and impeccably designed upholstered furniture, the blazing fire in the fireplace (though it's 85 degrees outside), and most of all, the security guys with little black earpieces who keep staring at me, all make me feel like I do not belong here. Any minute someone in a suit may approach and ask me why I have the audacity to use up their air when the luxurious rooms here cost over $800 a night.

There have been times in the last three decades when I have felt similar feelings in my church. Yes, we are far more egalitarian than most churches when it comes to our position and practice of placing women in key leadership roles. But as the first woman on the management team and the first woman teaching pastor, there have been moments when I wondered if I really belonged, if it is right and good for me to take a place at the table, if what appears to be an exclusive boys' club at times can make room for some girls. What has gotten me through, first and foremost, are the distinct whispers of the Spirit calling me to persevere and play the part he called me to play. But the other reason I'm still in leadership in the church can only be attributed to strong men who invited me onto their teams, and then made me feel like my contribution was welcome and mattered and could only grow and flourish. I owe them an enormous debt of gratitude because it would have been far easier for them to take the more common path and bar my entrance, along with the entrance of other women who followed.

You have a choice to make. You can push this issue aside, hope it goes away for a time, and keep focusing on all the other really big concerns at your church. Or you can keep listening and learning and make yourself available to be an agent for change. As part of your listening, you might even read through the rest of this book in an effort to understand the wider experience of women seeking to use their leadership gifts in the church. You can take a strong woman leader or a group of women leaders to lunch and free them up to reveal to you what they are concerned about. You can do your study and allow the Holy Spirit to impress on you where your church could make progress.

Without apology, I call you to be bold and courageous and diligent for the sake of your church and its future impact, for the sake of your own soul and your staff, and for the sake of all the women who linger on the sidelines, who wonder if there is a place for them, and who have such remarkable potential to soar. We are counting on you.

EIGHT

LEANING INTO YOUR TRIBE

A blank computer screen stared back at me, defying my efforts to think through a message I was attempting to write while sitting in a favorite coffee shop. It was a bright and beautiful morning in Chicago, with low humidity and warm temperatures beckoning me to sit outside.

Unfortunately, it's impossible to read a computer screen in blazing sunlight, so I forced myself to stay put. A few moments later, a group of women sat down with their lattes and mochas at one of the outdoor tables. I recognized several of them. After watching their interactions for awhile, I discerned they were having some kind of meeting, probably planning a school event, since they were all moms of kids around the same age, and were apparently making assignments as they chatted.

For nine o'clock in the morning, these women looked very put together, relaxed, and full of fun. I wrestled with feelings of envy, picturing what the rest of their day might look like — which I imagined included time to be a homemaker who actually gets errands done, creates a picture-perfect home and a delicious dinner for her family, has time to volunteer for school events, and even puts in a healthy workout at her local health club before getting a professional manicure. I engaged in one of those comparison games women sometimes play and pondered my own choices as a part-time working mom whose home is always in at least a mild state of chaos, who rarely offers any time to her daughters' schools, and whose family always asks the question, "What's for dinner?" with a bit of trepidation and a distinct lack of excitement.

That morning in the coffee shop provoked feelings in me that I admit to wrestling with here and there for many years, feelings about my own choices and the choices of other women I respect and admire. In the last two decades, much has been written about *mommy wars*, an undercurrent of judgment and hostility among women that pits those who choose to be full-time homemakers against those who choose to be employed outside the home. I wish I could say there are no mommy wars in ministry, that the church is a less divisive place for women with leadership gifts as they interact with other women, but sadly, that has not been my experience nor the picture described by others. Just as adolescents can be *mean girls*, grown-ups can turn into *mean women* who subtly—or not so subtly—undermine, judge, and criticize the choices of other women they worship next to on Sunday mornings. Those of us who lead in the church must zealously avoid making any contribution to the divisiveness of the mommy wars. Instead, we must intentionally develop and lean into our own circle—our tribe—of friends, and then turn around and invest in the young women who follow behind us.

No More Mommy Wars

Never before have there been so many options for women in terms of marriage, birth control, childcare, and employment. There are multiple scenarios for women to choose from, and all women make a variety of changes and choices as they navigate new seasons of life and are confronted with new realities. Most single mothers, for example, likely did not anticipate the life they are now living, and yet they courageously navigate the challenges of raising children on their own, or at least without a father living in the home. We all know women who invest themselves full-time in raising their children for an era, and who then reinvent themselves in the empty nest years. Some women are blissfully single adults, while others still hope marriage will be a part of their story. So if all these options and lifestyle choices exist, why is it so hard for us to learn how to accept and support the choices of others without resorting to a judgmental spirit that is overtly or covertly just plain mean?

I think the mommy war mind-set stems fundamentally from a deep-rooted insecurity that leads to the sins of envy and coveting. The definition of envy is "to be discontented at the possession of another of what one would like for oneself; malicious grudging." Coveting is basically a synonym for envy. We envy because there is a difference between who we are and who we feel we should be or who others insist we should be.

Just as adolescents can be mean girls, grown-ups can turn into mean women who subtly — or not so subtly — undermine, judge, and criticize the choices of other women they worship next to on Sunday mornings.

Our culture is obsessed with comparisons. In her excellent book, *The Snow White Syndrome*, Betsy Cohen writes that "we encourage everyone to earn more money, to look better, to do better, to learn more, to have more. Our society creates inevitable comparison and inevitable dissatisfaction."[19] God is so serious about the problem of envy that he specifically addresses coveting in the Ten Commandments (Ex. 20:17). And the letter from James boldly states that "where you have envy and selfish ambition, there you find disorder and every evil practice" (3:16).

Where does our envy come from and what can we do to combat this green-eyed monster? A professor at Purdue University, Robert Bringle, stresses that "we covet most strongly in areas important to our sense of self-worth." In other words, each of us is most susceptible to envy in the arenas in which we feel most vulnerable or weak. Women leaders who are not at peace with their identities or confident in the choices they have made can doubt themselves to the point that they tear down others in an effort to boost their own worth. Let me ask you this question: In what arenas do you find yourself most likely to become envious of other women? When we answer that question, we discern where perhaps we ourselves are most insecure.

When I ask myself such a question, I come up with an answer all too quickly. The area of my self-esteem that is most fragile centers on the domestic parts of life — cooking, gardening, home decorating, etc. Therefore, I am most likely to become envious around women I call the *Martha Stewarts* or the *Rachael Rays*. (My mother gave me a plaque for my kitchen that states, "Martha Stewart does not live here!") These are women who design and sew their own curtains, make their own candles, effortlessly whip up recipes straight out of *Bon Appétit*—you know the type. I have a few friends in this category, and then my brother turned around and married a Martha Stewart! Not only can Tami lovingly mother four children, create a fabulous home that could be featured in a magazine, sew costumes for her children's plays, and cook like Emeril Lagasse, but she also happens to be very nice! Tami is godly, loving, generous, fun, pretty—in short, she used to make me sick! I noticed that when my brother Chip first married Tami, I felt a little depressed after visiting their home. Seeing Tami's skills in action reminded me of all my inadequacy and failure in the domestic realm. I often used humor or sarcasm to mask what was truly the sin of envy in my heart.

A close examination of our inner responses as we encounter women who have made different choices can reveal whether we are struggling with coveting and insecurity. Here are some key questions to ponder:

- Do you tend to belittle the accomplishments, talents, or appearances of other women?
- Are you secretly upset when another woman advances professionally or socially? What is your response to her success?
- Are you tempted to bad-mouth or sabotage a person to whom you feel inferior?

- Are you secretly pleased when a woman colleague or friend suffers a setback?
- Do you find yourself making judgments and assumptions about the choices of other women leaders, particularly those who are mothers?
- Do you invest a lot of energy in comparing yourself to other women physically, intellectually, spiritually, and professionally?

Envy is such an embarrassing sin because it is petty and it creeps around with such subtlety that we often don't realize it's there until it has morphed into a simmering bitterness. In Proverbs we read, "Anger is cruel and fury overwhelming, but who can stand before jealousy?" (Prov. 27:4). What most concerns me about envy in the hearts of women leaders is that it wastes so much of our time, robs us of deep joy in our own uniqueness, and destroys the possibility for authentic and life-giving community. Our coveting creates distance between us and God and between us and others. When I am envious, I can't be truly grateful or productive because I am too busy feeling deprived. So what can we do to free ourselves from this devious sin and life-robbing pattern? Our path out of envy will require us to come out of hiding, redirect our thoughts and energy, and believe the best about other women.

Come out of Hiding

To deal with envy, we must first call it what it is and admit our sin. Dr. Joyce Brothers says that we are "so ashamed of envious feelings that we seldom pull them out into the light where we can get a good look at them."[20] Envy has many disguises. If you frequently find fault with others, if you feel a lack of joy and contentment, if you cannot truly rejoice with those who rejoice—examine your heart carefully. If what is really going on inside your heart is envy, admit that to be true, first of all to God. Say it out loud or write it down—"I feel envious." When we own up to our envy, we empower ourselves to move from confession to transformation. Often, it can be helpful to actually admit our coveting to another person, maybe even to the very target of our envy.

At some point I decided to own up to my envy of Tami, and to have a conversation with her about it. Taking that step was incredibly freeing for me. As often happens when women admit their coveting to one another, I discovered that there are aspects to my life that Tami admires and knows are not her strengths, such as speaking in public. She gracefully told me how her domestic gifts and passions have been true about her since she was a little girl, and they come so naturally and easily to her that she does not consider them to be a big deal (which is how it is with any gift). I felt like a burden came off my shoulders when I admitted my envy, and now I can go to Tami's house without feeling depressed or inadequate because I am free to celebrate the wonder of who she is and not focus so much on who I am not. I did wobble a bit the year we came for Christmas dinner and I saw how Tami marked our places at the table. I pat myself on the back if I use a part of an index card to indicate where people should sit, so obviously my standards are pretty lame. On that holiday on Tami's exquisitely set table, our names sat above each plate scripted in gingerbread — not only were they beautiful, but they were also *edible*! This almost put me over the edge, but I recovered. Living in a perpetual state of envy is destructive to our souls and destroys the possibility for community and joy.

If any of my words about envy have triggered a sense of conviction in your spirit, please be willing to put the book down and examine your own heart and mind for traces of envy. Until we bring our darkness out into the light, we cannot hope to be healed and freed. Ask yourself with unflinching specificity who you tend to envy, the kinds of women you tend to resent, and dig deep to discern the insecurities that lie at the root of your envy. You will be on your way to far more joy, gratitude, and authentic relationships as you untangle this deviously subtle sin from your soul and confess it to your Creator.

Redirect Your Thoughts and Energy

It takes mental discipline and a strong will to stop ourselves from making unhealthy and unproductive comparisons. Eleanor Roosevelt once said, "No one can make you feel inferior without your consent."[21] Train yourself to refrain from viewing people in some kind of hierarchy and remember that different means different, not necessarily better or worse. Leaders like me who struggle with perfectionism must embrace the truth that no one can be good at everything. Instead of caving in to endless cycles of comparison, I must accept the essence of my own strengths and then seek to improve whatever areas of weakness I can address. Moving past envy can be a tremendous stimulus for change, and a far better investment of our energies.

For example, if you often find yourself envying a woman who seems to have a devoted prayer life, apply your energies toward learning how she has cultivated that spiritual discipline, and maybe even ask her for some guidance and resources to help you grow in that area. Most of us can improve in several areas, but if the traits you envy are simply not attainable—for example, all the voice lessons in the world are not going to make me a singer—then work to come to a place of acceptance. I don't have to be good at everything, and I can learn to celebrate the awesome musical gifts of others.

This process of redirection requires me to have a firm grip on my own uniqueness and a sense of peace about my own choices. There are pros and cons to any lifestyle choices women make, and no one would describe her life as always blissfully easy or 100 percent joyful and fulfilling. When I am tempted to envy my friends who do not have children to care for at home because their lives seem so much less frantic and they have room for solitude and more rest, I remind myself of the reasons Warren and I chose to become parents, and of the joyful upsides of that decision. None of us can have it all all the time! I don't want to waste time and energy any longer in the comparison game. I'd much rather focus on living *my* best life because I get only one shot; there will only ever be one of me on this planet, and I long to hear from God that I did well with what he entrusted to me. At that moment in heaven, the Lord will not be comparing any of us to another — we will simply be called to account for how we invested what we were given. That is both freeing and sobering.

Believe the Best

The third essential way to rid ourselves of envy is to practice the art of believing the best about other women. Here is what I choose to think about any other woman and her choices:

I do not ever know the whole story.

Every woman is trying to do the best she can.

This pattern of thought is especially helpful for those women leaders who are mothers and are tempted to judge and evaluate other women leaders who are mothers, because this is the arena in which so much envy and judgment seems to occur. Every mom has a story — what goes on in her own home in terms of the role, if any, played by the father, the financial situation, the health of family members, the unique needs of each child, and the amount of help available from extended family. Every mom works with a unique and highly specific set of conditions, and is doing the best she can for her family. Moms who choose to work outside the home love their children every bit as much as full-time homemakers, and work for a host of different reasons. It is never my job or my place to evaluate those choices, and when I find myself tempted to judge, I must ask myself what need in me prompts such unhealthy thoughts. Am I trying to bolster my own choices? Am I trying to bring that woman down a notch in my own mind? Am I too quick to make assumptions that may be very far off the mark if I only knew the whole story? What if I would choose to believe the best about that woman's intentions and her commitment to Christ, to her family, and to the church?

I believe we can thrive in deep and life-giving community with one another if we are all willing to lay down our subtle but deadly knives of envy and judgment, to let go of our need to somehow set the standard or parameters of *what every woman should do.* We need to simply *stop this madness* and celebrate the fact that there are so many options, so many wonderful and unique stories, so many ways for women these days to live their best lives and make a contribution to their families, to their friends, to their churches, and to the world. I invite you to join me in the parade of those women who give God praise for the diversity among us and who are far more quick to defend and support one another than to tear one another down. Will you be a part of that kind of revolution?

When we come out of hiding and stop masking our envy, when we redirect our thoughts and energies beyond the relentless cycle of comparison, and when we choose to believe the best about one another, we have a chance to actually win—all of us can win. Being a woman leader in the church is hard enough without trying to do it alone, distrusting or demeaning the very sisters in Christ who could actually provide us with understanding, support, refuge, mutual challenge, and encouragement. That's why I believe we must build and lean into a tribe.

It Takes a Tribe

Few conversations sadden me more than the ones I have with women leaders who feel terribly isolated as they try to invest their gifts in the church. If I am speaking over the phone to such a woman, everything in me wishes I could immediately transport myself into her presence, share a cup of tea, and give her a hug. None of us was designed to face the challenges of ministry alone, and though most leaders are surrounded by lots of people, women leaders too often lack the kind of soulish sisters with whom they can safely vent their frustrations, ask their questions, and wrestle with the unique challenges that emerge in any church setting.

Because many women tend to care for everyone else before addressing their own personal needs, not enough women leaders have granted themselves permission to spend time forming and building a tribe of other women. In her inspiring book, *Nice Girls Don't Change the World*, Lynne Hybels declares that the best thing she ever did was to "tiptoe out of isolation and join the circle of women ... When we do this, when we help one another, cheer one another on, call one another to our truest and highest selves, we become a powerful force for good — for God — in this world."[22]

I doubt I would have made it this far in ministry without the women in my tribe. Recently, I had a rare and remarkable experience with several members of my tribe to celebrate a significant birthday milestone. (I'm not saying which one!) My husband gave me the gift of inviting key women from my life to join me for a weekend at a condo in Florida. We shared a magical time laughing poolside with piles of magazines and our Diet Cokes, exploring the local shops, eating tremendous meals together, and simply hanging out. I have always cherished a fantasy that certain close friends of mine would surely love and click with other close friends of mine (from out of state) if only they were brought together. That fantasy came true! My girlfriends quickly liked one another and I basked in the joy of watching them connect.

> *Please don't try to be a lone ranger in leadership or in life — when the inevitable storms blow, you will desperately require the reinforcement of other women who know you well.*

On our final morning together, I looked around the room at the loving eyes of these women. God has used them to meet various needs in my life, to shore me up in a variety of ways. I saw Polly, my longest friend from childhood, with whom I have shared all kinds of losses and victories with the treasured knowledge that she knows me as well or better than anyone, because she knows where I come from and has walked with me all along. I saw Lynn and Karla, my mom friends, without whom I can't imagine dealing with the challenges of everyday life. I saw

Suze and Caron, two women who are leaders at their churches, who both listen to me and give me their amazing gifts of objectivity, wisdom, laughter, and hope. They frequently remind me that I'm not crazy and they love me far more than I deserve. I thought of those who could not join us that weekend — Corinne, Sue, and Nancy O. — and I sent up a prayer of gratitude for my friends. *God, I am a rich woman whom you have blessed with unbelievable friends who contribute immeasurably to my life. Thank you with all my heart!*

If you feel envious as you read about the friends in my tribe, redirect your energy and think about your own situation. If you lack a tribe, begin by assessing candidates. Are there any women you feel safe enough with to begin building a closer friendship, either inside or outside your church? You most likely need both, because sometimes you can't reveal your concerns appropriately to those in your own church community. Initiate a breakfast or lunch with one of these women, and taste what the connection feels like. You may need to get together a few times before you know whether this is a friendship with potential to be mutually worth your time and effort.

But be assured that building a tribe requires time. Friendships must be cultivated, nurtured, and paid attention to. We can't microwave a tribe, much as we wish we could. I learned early on in ministry that time with friends would cost me, but the payoffs far outweigh the sacrifice. Please don't try to be a lone ranger in leadership or in life — when the inevitable storms blow, you will desperately require the reinforcement of other women who know you well, who can speak truth to you with love, who will show up no matter what. If you are married, do not place the entire weight of your relational needs on your husband. No matter how great a guy he may be, that is too heavy a burden for anyone. There are frequent situations in which only a member of my tribe can truly understand me.

Think about your next big birthday milestone. If you were to celebrate it with a tribe of friends, do you know who you would invite? How many would you hope to include? Most importantly, are you making regular investments in crafting friendships so you are shored up and strong, so you can say with confidence that you are not alone, and so you can give and receive a deep and abiding kind of love to a few others? I long for every woman leader to thrive in a tribe, and then to turn her attention toward the next generation of women who are looking for guidance and support.

A Call for Mentors

With the shortage of women leaders in both the corporate world and in our churches, one would think that those who are in leadership would be the most passionate and intentional advocates for other women to emerge in key roles. Sadly, this is often not the case. For some reason, women who have achieved a level of influence sometimes make it even harder for other women to soar. It's as though we have a scarcity mentality and are afraid there won't be enough room for more than one effective female leader around our table. Perhaps our lack of support stems from an even darker place of hoarding the influence, holding on too tightly to the uniqueness of being the only woman on a team, or fear that another woman leader might surpass us with her gifts and accomplishments. This is the ugly truth in too many of our churches.

For a few years, I was the only woman teaching pastor at my church. Then John Ortberg and his, wife, Nancy moved to the Chicago area to join our team, and Nancy eventually was asked to lead Axis, our ministry to twentysomethings. Before long it became obvious to everyone that Nancy was an outstanding leader and communicator. She built a remarkable team of young leaders, empowering them to discover their sweet spot in ministry, freeing them to dream and to create. As a result of her leadership, Axis flourished. In addition, Nancy's teaching was widely appreciated, so she was asked to join our small team of teaching pastors. The Willow staff began to distinguish between us by referring to us as *Nancy O.* or *Nancy B.* — even our middle names are the same; we're both *Nancy Lee's*!

Inside me there was just a flicker of pause, wondering how it would feel to have another woman on the teaching team, tempted to compare myself to Nancy O., hesitant about whether there was enough room for both of us to minister with strength. But those little doubts and moments of insecurity quickly dissipated because of the mutual respect, growing friendship, and common understanding Nancy and I shared. I can honestly say, with great joy, that we became one another's biggest fans. We rarely taught a message without the other one sending a note of encouragement or affirming the other in person as we walked off the platform. The best part of all was that I no longer felt so alone. Nancy O. is a rare member of my tribe because we both get what it's like to try to minister on a primarily male team, what it's like to raise children and partner with a husband who is also full throttle in ministry. When the Ortbergs moved away to lead a ministry in the San Francisco Bay Area, I don't know anyone at Willow who cried harder or who misses them more than me. Recently, Nancy and I seized the opportunity to have lunch in another city where we were both asked to teach. The time flew by as we caught up with one another. Looking in her eyes, I see nothing but support, encouragement, humility, grace, and absolute delight celebrating whatever wins I have in my own journey.

We need to be able to say, "I'm so happy for you!" to another woman leader without gritting our teeth. It helps me to view my friends' victories as, in a sense, also my victories. When it comes to serving God and building the kingdom, there is more than enough room for all of us. In Numbers 11, we read of a situation in which Moses had an opportunity to hoard leadership or to celebrate the gifts of others. Joshua, Moses' protective protégé, rushes in to report that some other leaders are prophesying. Joshua wanted Moses to be the only teacher in the limelight. But Moses didn't feel threatened or insecure; his calm reply to Joshua was, " 'Are you jealous for my sake? I wish that all the LORD's people

> *When it comes to serving God and building the kingdom, there is more than enough room for all of us.*

were prophets and that the LORD would put his Spirit on them!'"
(Num. 11:29). Rather than trying to monopolize power or giftedness, we ought to cultivate the same gracious spirit as Moses.
Moses saw the big picture and longed for God to be strong at work
through many servants. In God's kingdom, shared accomplishments are more significant than individual achievements.

So how can women leaders move to a place of mutual support
and advocacy for others, including those who are just beginning?
At least part of the answer to that question centers on the role of
intentional mentoring. *Mentoring* is a big word, with a variety of
definitions and connotations attached to it depending on who is
doing the defining. For me, the concept of mentoring started out
feeling a little hard to pin down—what does it really mean to be a
mentor? Then a few years ago, I sensed a desire to build into some
of the emerging young women leaders on our staff, whether or not
they served in my area of ministry. I felt a strong prompting from
the Holy Spirit to carve out some time for these women, to invite
them to gather with me periodically.

At first I resisted this leading because I did not feel qualified to
be any kind of mentor. I felt that I still required mentoring myself
and was afraid none of these young women would even be all that
interested in spending time with me. But the promptings persisted.
So I asked around, thought about women I had already observed
and enjoyed, and initiated some phone calls. Eventually, I invited
about nine of them to join me every other Friday afternoon for
about ninety minutes. I had no idea what I was doing! Still, we
ended up calling this our mentoring group, and I tried to figure
out how to invest the time wisely, along with other opportunities to
meet with them individually.

I can't stop smiling when I think about that group of young
women, all in their twenties, most of them single, all of them with
shining eyes and contagious energy and delightful spunk. Heather,
Jill, Shauna, Holly, Annie, Mindy, Jeanne, Deirdre, and Ashley. We
sat in various rooms in the church for our meetings, and I tried to

figure out how to structure and guide our time. There were gatherings in which we discussed a book I had asked them all to read about leadership, but most often I would raise an issue or describe a kind of situation or simply respond to their perceptive questions. They wanted to explore how to manage their personal lives as much as how to grow in their leadership skills, so our conversations sometimes felt like they were unfocused and all over the map. I am quite certain I could have led them better, but I truly was making all this up as we went along. Eventually, I realized that what mattered most was being together, the interest I showed in their lives and their ideas and their challenges, and the ways they also helped one another and built into me. We met for about three years, swapping in a few new women when some had to leave for one reason or another. But the nucleus of the group stayed the same.

I have watched several of those young women get married and give birth to their first children. These days they are all serving in some form of ministry, and I am thrilled to cheer them from the sidelines. I still don't know very much about mentoring, but I do know this—all of us, no matter what our age, have something of worth to offer other women. This intentional investment can begin even for young girls in high school who lead a small group of middle schoolers! There is something truly life-giving about a woman who is just a little further along giving the gift of her time, attention, and growing wisdom to another woman. This investment can range widely from a casual series of appointments at the local coffee shop with just one other woman to a more formalized kind of group setting.

It helps us to be less daunted by the concept of mentoring if we recognize that none of us can provide all the guidance needed by a protégé. Speaker and writer Lynette Lewis, in her book *Climbing the Ladder in Stilettos*, describes the importance of mentoring moments. Whether we are seeking a mentor for our own purposes or considering the possibility to mentor someone else, we can right-size our expectations. Lewis states: "Rather than expect one or two individuals to meet one-on-one with us regularly, we should instead look for moments of exchange with people who offer nuggets of wisdom that we can apply."[23]

Most of us look back at our lives and appreciate the brief mentoring we have received from a variety of men and women who, at a certain point in time, spoke the needed word into our lives or provided us with a living example to emulate. Rarely are any of us blessed with the perfect, all-encompassing mentor who can build into every dimension of our lives. Instead we treasure smaller encounters with other leaders and glean whatever we can from their investment in us, regardless of the length of time we enjoyed their presence.

I am still stunned by the thirst for mentoring I see in the next generation of leaders, both men and women. When a younger leader contacts me and asks for the gift of my time, I am honored and also sobered by the responsibility. In many ways I believe the next season of my life is primarily going to focus on giving back, passing the baton to young leaders who are full of potential and passion, and simply offering any bits of wisdom I have

The older I get, the more I regret any energy I wasted comparing myself with other women, being envious of them, or feeling insecure about my own choices.

learned along the way. Mentoring will not happen by accident. We must be intentional, open, always looking for opportunities to give a word of encouragement, making time for unrushed conversations, breathing life and hope and exhortation and comfort into the souls of others. Few investments are more rewarding.

How intentional are you about investing in the lives of women leaders who are just a bit behind you in their experience? Can you think of some names for potential mentoring candidates and prayerfully begin to initiate dialogue with them? If you detect even a hint of the scarcity mentality, an insecurity about making a place for other women who may possibly display more gifts or exert more influence than you, be honest about your feelings and do the hard work of rooting them out. There truly is more than enough room for all of us, and the kingdom will not advance unless we are willing to humbly turn around and lend a hand to raise up the leaders of tomorrow.

The older I get, the more I regret any energy I wasted comparing myself with other women, being envious of them, or feeling insecure about my own choices. The truth is that when we stop the mommy wars and choose to believe the best about one another, we have the chance to do life in a tribe of women who contribute in immeasurable ways to the joy and adventure of the journey. I don't want to sit in coffee shops doing my work, watching women who are primarily full-time homemakers, and do anything else but celebrate the fact that we all get to paint our own lives and that every painting can be beautiful and entirely unique. Every season of our lives will be different, whether or not we are moms, whether or not we are married, whether or not we bring home a paycheck. What never changes is the need for authentic, life-giving community with one another. Refuse to do this journey alone. We need one another, and those who come after us require our attention as well. So please, commit to forming and leaning into your very own tribe. The adventure will be so much sweeter.

· CONCLUSION ·

The road for women leading and teaching in the church is not usually a smooth one, and is often fraught with a mixture of frustration, hurt, anger, challenge, new opportunities, joy, and deep fulfillment. Each woman wakes up every day to a unique set of challenges and joys and must navigate an authentic path through her own life—both at home and in the church. But no matter how hard it sometimes gets, without apology I offer three final words to my sisters in the ministry: *Fulfill your calling*. This is the spirit of the instructions Paul gave to Timothy when he wrote, "But you, be sober in all things, endure hardship, do the work of an evangelist, fulfill your ministry" (2 Tim. 4:5 NASB).

Calling is a profound word, and a concept that can feel overwhelming as we seek to discern what precisely God calls us to do, where he wants us to live it out, and how to maximize the gifts entrusted to us. If you are like me, when the obstacles present themselves, I am far too quick to fantasize about abandoning that calling and taking a far cushier path—like maybe living on a beach somewhere and reading piles of books to my heart's content. I have what Gordon MacDonald refers to as a "quitter's gene" in me, beckoning me on a daily basis to give up the struggle and take it easy.

But when I'm tempted to quit, I recall the face of a woman I'll never forget, a woman my husband and I encountered decades ago on an island just off the coast of Haiti. After visiting some ministries in the poverty-stricken city of Port au Prince, I thought nothing could be much worse than the devastating conditions we encountered there—sheetrock shacks with no sanitary systems, waste in the streets, children hanging onto our legs begging for a piece of bread, pregnant mothers who had already lost multiple children to starvation looking me in the eyes as if to say, "How will I be able to feed this one in my belly?" It was a wrenching experience. Then we took a short plane ride to La Gonaves, a small island just a few miles away. There we encountered a small mission built on ground so hard that nothing grew in it. We saw no trees, heard no birds, observed no way a family could grow food or sustain themselves. My husband could not help but notice that the children had no toys to play with, nothing to offer a respite from their hunger and boredom. It was beastly hot, and the island had no source of power except for a rickety generator that provided unreliable electricity for a few hours each day.

The woman who led the mission greeted us with a warm smile. She had lived on that island as a missionary for over thirty years. *Thirty years.* I still cannot get my mind and heart around that kind of sacrifice. The few hours I visited the island seemed like a week, and I longed for my air-conditioned hotel room and a refreshing shower. But this woman loved the small community of people on that island. She was fiercely devoted to them. She did not have to stay there—anyone would have understood if she one day decided that *enough is enough.* But she persevered and, for all I know, may still be there, fulfilling her calling, making a difference for God.

I look forward to reuniting with that sister in heaven someday, along with all the other sisters who choose on planet earth to faithfully invest their time and energy using the gifts God gave them to advance the kingdom. We must not allow hardships to create excuses for becoming less than God designed for us to be. If we believe that no mistake was made in heaven when our gifts were assigned, then we must wake up each morning with a renewed commitment to do the best we can with what we have been given.

I pray that our Creator has used the words of this book to make you feel a little less alone. I hope what I've written has helped you to feel recognized and understood by another woman who is still trying to figure it out, trying to fulfill her own calling, not getting it right much of the time, but also recognizing and celebrating progress and hope. As you seek to penetrate the awkwardness of the boys' club, to balance the unbelievable challenges of ministry with a vital and meaningful personal life, and as you lean into a tribe of other women for mutual support and burden sharing, may you hear the encouraging whispers of the Holy Spirit. In fact, if I may be so bold, I believe the Lord wants you to know that he is exceedingly proud of you—of your courage and tenacity and grace. You are a precious daughter of the Most High God. So don't give up. Write your own story, and one day we can compare notes over a cup of tea (okay, coffee if you must) in heaven. Fulfill your calling, or in words I mean with all my heart, *You go girl!*

· AFTERWORD ·

For My Daughters
(and other young women growing up in the church)

Dear Samantha and Johanna,

In many ways I wrote this book for you, my precious daughters. One of the most tremendous and daunting privileges of my life has been the gift of being your mom. All three of us know, without a doubt, that I have made countless mistakes as a mother, and I hope I've said "I'm sorry" for at least most of them. You both figured out a long time ago that I would not be the mom who crafted the winning Halloween costume, cooked up the most delicious gourmet meals, organized your photos into elegantly designed memory books, or received ribbons for being a Room Mom at school. I hope you also know that I tried to lean into my strengths as a woman and as a mom, and did the job the only way I knew how to do it. Above all, I have loved you ferociously.

I take absolute delight in observing who both of you are becoming and in celebrating your many gifts. From toddlerhood, you both blazed with creativity, always excited by your favorite phrase, "Let's pretend!" I will forever cherish all the little shows, dances, plays, and productions you put together in our basement and, later, on stages at church and at school. Your father and I are front-row witnesses to the passion that lies within you to tell a story, to create characters, and to communicate with your bodies and voices through the arts.

You are also leaders, evident from your earliest years. Samantha, your preschool teacher told me that in her multiple decades of early childhood education, she had never seen a little boy or little girl lead so effectively, rallying the class with energy, and also with tremendous kindness. Johanna, your leadership came to light in grammar school, when you were elected president of the student council, among other key roles. I love watching how your friends respect and follow you, how you lead with grace and exhibit early signs of relational intelligence.

Of course, you are individuals, and not identical to one another. It will bring your father and me great joy, Jo, to see where your fantastic eye for visual design will lead you, and Sam, how your gift of writing will play out in the future. You have both been blessed with sharp minds, a sense of humor, and an ability to make others feel included and appreciated. When combined with your Christlike character, these traits have the potential to enable you to make a difference in this world, to contribute to the cause of Christ as you serve others. I have no idea yet what your specific contributions will be, and I certainly hope to live long enough to get a glimpse and cheer you on.

You have so many options. My fervent hope is that while you examine all your choices, while you sort through your strengths and admit your weaknesses, and most of all, while you listen for the whispers of the Holy Spirit, you will carefully consider making a mark in a local church. Your role could be on staff or as a volunteer — that really is not the point. But I long for you to invest yourselves in the ministry of a local church community, to show up with your quick minds, your loving hearts, and your childlike creativity. The church desperately needs young women like you — to lead, to strategize, to teach, to design, to write, to act, to dance.

I will not paint a picture for you that is inaccurate or too pretty; investing your gifts in the church is most likely not the easiest path you could take. Certainly I hope that through women leaders before me, through my generation and the one that follows, more doors will be nudged open for you that were previously shut. If any of us who have preceded your generation modeled a way for women in church to lead and to teach, we are deeply honored to have played a part. But my guess is that in many churches, it will still be a challenge for you to take a seat at the table. You may find yourself in a culture that still resembles more of a boys' club. But don't let that hold you back if God is guiding you forward. We need you young women—oh, how we need you.

The church truly is the hope of the world. You've heard me say that many times. But please know that I believe it with every fiber of my being. The future of the church lies in the hands of young leaders like you. As you prayerfully seek direction on how to invest your one and only life, please know that the kingdom of God will advance only if and when individuals called by God courageously and enthusiastically show up with all they are and all they have, ready and willing to serve and persevere for the cause of Christ. Whether you serve the under-resourced like your father does, toiling in the inner city or in a remote African village, or whether you write stories to tell on Sunday mornings—or teach messages, or lead a team of young people, or rally artists to give their very best for God—no matter what your specific calling, fulfill your ministry. Don't let anything hold you back, and celebrate that God crafted you as a woman.

Here's a little dream I have—that one day you will both have daughters too, and that maybe you will show them, several years from now, this little book. "Your grandmother wrote this," you will tell your girls. "The book is quite outdated now. Believe it or not, at one time not long ago, women found it somewhat difficult to lead in the church. They felt sometimes like their gifts were not welcome, and so your grandma wrote a book to let them know they were not alone, and that God didn't make a mistake when he entrusted them with their gifts of leadership and teaching."

"Wow. That's weird." And off they will run to play and to soar and to become whatever it is God intends for them to become.

With a heart full of love and gratitude,
Your Mom

· APPENDIXES ·

Additional Resources

"Voice," by Jane Stephens

Statement on Women and Men in Leadership:
Willow Creek Community Church

FAQs

◆ Appendix 1 ◆

Additional
Resources

For Theological/Scriptural Study

Listed here is just a small sample of the many resources available on the subject of men and women in ministry. For a more comprehensive list of resources, see the appendix of Dr. Gilbert Bilezikian's book, *Beyond Sex Roles*.

Belleville, Linda L.; Blomberg, Craig L.; Keener, Craig S.; Schriener, Thomas R. *Two Views on Women in Ministry.* **Grand Rapids: Zondervan, 2001, 2005.**

Edited by James R. Beck, this book offers essays from four contributors: two egalitarian and two complementarian. What is most helpful and unique is that the revised edition includes critiques on each essay from the other three authors, allowing for comparison and contrast on key points of scholarship and interpretation.

Bilezikian, Gilbert. *Beyond Sex Roles: A Guide for the Study of Female Roles in the Bible.* **Grand Rapids: Baker, 1985.**

This study of women's roles explores the progressive revelation and will of God from creation through the fall to redemption. Carefully unpacking each of the relevant Scripture passages, the author offers scriptural confirmation for no discrimination in church and family life. Extensive endnotes dig even deeper into the challenging theological questions, with a focus on a contrasting work by James B. Hurley, *Men and Women in Biblical Perspective.*

Bilezikian, Gilbert. *Community 101: Reclaiming the Local Church as Community of Oneness.* **Grand Rapids: Zondervan, 1997.**

A call to live out a biblical vision of community, this book includes thorough treatment of the role of women in the church, particularly in the third chapter, "Ministry."

Grenz, Stanley J. and Kjesbo, Denise Muir. *Women in the Church: A Biblical Theology of Women in Ministry.* **Downers Grove, Ill.: InterVarsity, 1995.**

Hurley, James B. *Man and Woman in Biblical Perspective.* **Grand Rapids: Zondervan, 1981.**

This work represents the most significant arguments used in support of the complementarian pattern for male/female relationships in church and family life. In extensive notes in the back of his book, *Beyond Sex Roles*, Gilbert Bilezikian comments on key sections of Hurley's work.

Kimball, Dan. *They Like Jesus but Not the Church.* **Grand Rapids: Zondervan, 2007.**

Chapter 7 explores the perspective of the emerging, non-churched generation toward the issue of women in leadership.

McKnight, Scot. *Blue Parakeet: Rethinking How You Read the Bible.* **Grand Rapids: Zondervan, 2008.**

An entire section of this book is devoted to providing guidance on how to read Scripture when it comes to the issue of women in ministry. Scot McKnight, professor of religious studies at North Park University, tells the story of his own journey—from a fundamentalist background to being an avid supporter of women in church leadership. His theological and biblical observations are solid and extremely valuable to this discussion.

Ortberg, John. *What the Bible Says about Men and Women,* **four-part message series; available as MP3s, audio CDs, or transcripts from the Willow Creek Association (www.willowcreek.com), 1999.**

Sumner, Sarah. *Men and Women in the Church: Building Consensus on Christian Leadership.* **Downers Grove, Ill.: InterVarsity, 2003.**

For Moms

Though not written from a Christian perspective, these books are written by women who offer helpful perspectives on their personal experience and the experience of other women navigating the challenges of motherhood and work outside the home.

Krasnow, Iris. *Surrendering to Motherhood.* **New York: Hyperion, 1997.**

This author transitioned from a highly demanding career to mothering four young boys. I appreciated her honesty about her journey and discoveries along the way.

Marshall, Melinda M. *Good Enough Mothers: Changing Expectations for Ourselves.* **Princeton, N.J.: Peterson's, 1993.**

This book was extremely helpful to me as I wrestled with unrealistic expectations and unhealthy guilt for working outside the home. Marshall helped me to slay my "Perfect Mother Monster."

Walsh, Elsa. *Divided Lives: The Public and Private Struggles of Three Accomplished Women.* **New York: Simon & Schuster, 1995.**

Walsh spent over two years interviewing women about their lives, and she examines their choices as they sought balance in their lives. The primary focus of the book centers on three extraordinary women.

For Women in Leadership

Fiorina, Carly. *Tough Choices.* **New York: Penguin, 2006.**

As the first female CEO of Hewlett Packard, Carly Fiorina experienced numerous challenges, including some connected to her gender. This is an honest and highly engaging memoir.

Frankel, Lois P. *See Jane Lead: 99 Ways for Women to Take Charge at Work.* **New York: Warner Business Books, 2007.**

Dr. Frankel is a consultant on leadership development and team building. Her book is full of practical strategies and insights for the everyday work of leadership.

Hybels, Lynne. *Nice Girls Don't Change the World.* **Grand Rapids: Zondervan, 2005.**

Lynne tells her compelling story of moving from trying to meet what she thought were the expectations of God, her husband, the church, and others, to living out the unique gifts and passions God has given her. Her story inspires all of us to reach our full potential as women.

Lewis, Lynette. *Climbing the Ladder in Stilettos.* **Nashville: W Publishing Group, 2006.**

Lewis has navigated an eclectic career from PR and fundraising at a major university, to a role as a senior marketing leader. Writing from her perspective as a Christian woman in business, she offers a go-to guide for life as a woman in the working world.

"VOICE"
BY JANE STEPHENS

Vocation ... the place where our deep gladness and the world's deep hunger meet.

Frederick Buechner

Voice. You can't buy it at the store, but it is fundamental to great business and inspiring leadership. It is the litmus test of organizational values. An environment that asks people to solve problems with rote efficiency, to do the same thing over and over, finds voice unnecessary and disruptive. An environment committed to the cultivation of new ideas, markets, products, processes, and services finds it productive. Voice is the variable that explodes the scarcity model of economics—when you use it, you end up with more, and everyone can use it.

What is voice? It's hard to define. Watch a Nike commercial or read a poem by Maya Angelou and you'll probably hear it; read the manual for your dishwasher and you probably won't. Bob Dole had it on *Saturday Night Live*; he didn't when he ran for President. It occurs more often in E-mail than in year-end reports, but it's not really related to form, nor is it governed by audience. It begins with one's ability to own oneself, and it grows with one's ability to give that self to the world. It thrives at the cusp of those two experiences.

*Appendix 2 from Jane Stephens and Stephen Zades, *Mad Dogs, Dreamers, and Sages: Growth in the Age of Ideas* (New York: Elounda Press, 2003), 91–107.

Voice goes two ways. It's about learning to get in touch, listen to and trust your own instincts; it's about threading instinct and experience into the fulcrum of sharp, clear expression. Born at the intersection of tentativity and certainty, it requires both vulnerability and presence. It is the productive first ingredient for individuality and for collaboration, essential not only for changing the world, but for changing oneself.

Voice is an artesian well, the best resource of each person. Their most genuine, vital expression and energy, fueling the organization's best and wisest work. It happens when we are working at the center of our vocation — our calling, "the place where our own deep gladness meets the world's deep need."

Leaders need to find their own voices, their own best resources for being genuine in the midst of their organization, and they need to invite and to host the fullest presence of their colleagues. To have voice is to be fully present, to feel counted in, and counted on, to have something to say, and to be heard. The payoff for working in an organization in which everyone brings real voice to their work is a full measure of energy, balance, understanding, and fun.

Finding Voice

One afternoon in Nairobi, I visited with a Masaii woman, a princess. Her father was the tribal chief, and she was one of a hundred brothers and sisters, children of his ten wives. I marveled at her sense of grace and dignity as we talked about growing up with ninety-nine siblings. Her husband came into the yard and as she walked over to meet him, she knelt down and swooped up a handful of grass. Later she explained, "A Masaii woman always offers grass before she speaks. How can you speak if you come empty-handed?"

A big part of finding our own voice is realizing that we don't come empty-handed. Unfortunately, in our urgency to bring something of our own to the workplace conversation, our reach is often too shallow. We offer the shrill voice of false confidence, the chatter of emptiness, the sigh of indifference, or the hollow echo of gossip. What is it then that we can swoop up before we speak to make our offering worthy?

We've all had moments when to our own surprise we find ourselves speaking with power and confidence about something we've thought about for a long time, but never thought we'd talk about. Or even more surprising, we find ourselves speaking with insight and conviction about something we never thought we'd care about in the first place.

Something provokes or engages us; a door gets opened and suddenly we begin to talk. Not small talk or business talk or chitchat, but real talk about things we've discovered, observed, and considered. The power of our own voice surprises us. Something has been turned on. We are now working and thinking in a faster, fuller way.

What happened? Usually one of two things. Either another person made it clear that he truly wanted to hear what we thought, or something inside of us decided it could not go on being unheard any longer. When we expect everyone to bring their handful of grass, we give one another permission to be heard.

Built into the fabric of many companies are an array of gestures, assumptions, and arrangements that give our whole work force a sense that what they have to bring to the feast is minimal or optional, or that it is only necessary on demand. We need full-spirited people, not sometimes, but all the time. We need to leave the power running. Imagine the magnification of energy and exchange. A family of a hundred princes and princesses reaping a rich harvest in a desert land!

What Makes Voice Real?

What makes for real talk? It's not certainty. In fact, if we know exactly what we're going to say, it may well be unreal, borrowed from old ideas or someone else's repertoire. When we feel unheard in a job or relationship, we begin talking to ourselves about it — too much. The words we don't get to say out loud get a grip on our mind. As we're mowing the grass or driving down the highway, we find ourselves rehearsing a litany of *should have saids* and *could have saids* over and over.

We imagine these words as the speech we're going to make in our exit interview, the final great truth we'll pronounce as we're walking out the door. But real truth doesn't get told that way. We cannot save up our real voice and best thoughts to drop in a neat package as we're leaving: *The extra disks are in the drawer, the keys are in the mailbox, and, by the way, I never liked the way you ran the office.*

Real voice is the experience of speaking and *not* leaving. Of saying what we know and feeling it ring true all the way down to our shoes, and continuing to stand in them. Of feeling strong as we stand and hearing the words and meanings that come back to us as we're standing strong in our own voice.

It involves not a turning away from power, responsibility, and community, but a turning toward it. It works as a centrifugal force, pulling all of our disparate ideas towards the center, rather than centripetal, casting them outward. It may begin with a whisper, *Well, I was thinking about it this way* ... or *I'm not sure I feel right about that* ... or *I'd like to try to do it this way* ... but it carries far, gaining power as it goes.

Different Voices

Creating workplaces, organizations, and families that ask people to bring their full measure of self to work requires an honest audit of the range of selves we are prepared to host. Psychologist Carol Gilligan began to uncover the ways that academic research systems had failed to allow for a genuine range of voices while she was teaching at Harvard in the early 1970's. Working as a graduate assistant for psychologists Erik Erikson, a ground-breaking thinker on the development of identity, and Lawrence Kohlberg, a pioneer in the science of moral development, Gilligan began to notice that the young women she was studying didn't fit the categories Erikson and Kohlberg had developed.

Gilligan was particularly interested in the way the women in her studies differed in their approach to moral dilemmas from the men in Kohlberg's work. The content of their responses was different, but even more interesting to Gilligan, and harder to assess with the traditional tools of scientific method, was the way they used—or failed to use—their voices.

Written at the epicenter of feminism, the great tsunami of our times—when large numbers of women were entering into professional, political, and academic arenas—Gilligan's work was revolutionary. When her book, *In a Different Voice: Psychological Theory and Women's Development,* came out in 1982, it called for a complete recalibration of the study of human behavior. Since then it has sold close to a million copies in multiple languages; thousands of dissertations have been derived from it; books have been written about it and more books have been written about those books. It's a song everyone gets now. Sort of.

Despite tectonic shifts in the ways that every field has had to reconsider its assumptions in order to accommodate women's ways of knowing, Gilligan feels the most significant aspect of her breakthrough work has gone untapped. For her, more than any issue of gender, her studies reveal enormous gaps in all of our ability to speak and hear in our real voices.

In overlooking the power of voice as a measure of and source for ways of knowing and transforming ourselves and others, we are not only overlooking women, we are reducing reality. If, as Gilligan proposes, voice is the mother lode for human growth and social transformation and we can't buy it or teach it, both businesses and universities must address themselves better to the task of understanding it.

Joe McCarthy on Finding Real Voice As a Brand

The value of idea-driven businesses will largely be determined by the uniqueness, style, and power of real voice, and their ability to access and cultivate it throughout the organization. The independent visions of great business creators, Stephen Jobs of Apple, Yvonne Chanard of Patagonia, Jeff Bezos of Amazon.com, and Ralph Lauren of Polo are rich with voice. Each one has a *signature* voice, as does every vibrant person we know, be she a musician, CEO, physician, teacher, manager, parent, or friend. A real voice cuts through the fog of bureaucratic language in a way no other force can.

Advertising often seems like annoying clutter. Numbing words awash in a sea of sameness: *Buy me, fly me, try me please or else I'll badger you everywhere—don't think you can escape, I know where you live!* But at its best, advertising is the business of discovering voice.

Every once in awhile, a real voice breaks through; it's just different. A product or company moves you in a gripping, emotional way. Nike is an organization that seems to break through more often than most. To understand the connection between finding voice as an individual, as difficult as that can be, and finding voice as an organization, we went to Joe McCarthy who steered the global advertising division of Nike during the mid nineties when it redefined the depth and reach of brand voice for the rest of business.

You may remember some of the work from Nike's team, a black-and-white documentary montage of girls saying:

> If you let me play sports, I will like myself more. If you let me play, I will be more self-confident. If you let me play, I will be 60 percent less likely to get breast cancer, I will suffer less depression. If you let me play sports, I will be more likely to leave a man who beats me. If you let me play, I will be less likely to get pregnant before I want to. I will learn what it means to be strong, if you let me play sports.

Or watching Ric Muñoz as he runs through a park in Los Angeles:

> Eighty miles every week. Ten marathons every year. HIV positive.

At a time when violence against women was only beginning to be linked to societal factors, and gay athletes and HIV were still in the closet, Nike told the truth about investment and courage—and told it in a compelling and unsentimental way. When you get it right, it reverberates for years.

The soul of the brand

McCarthy gave us his best clues for discerning and developing brand with voice:

Find the soul. The essence of the brand that goes beyond its physical look and the target market is its soul. Soul even goes beyond the heart and the emotional connection. You just *know* when people or things have soul. It's the difference between Marvin Gaye and Michael Bolton.

Be true to your core values. The spirit of Nike is performance and authenticity. The spirit of Johnson & Johnson is trust and confidence. Unless marketers fully understand the core values of their brand as the basis for all decisions about the brand, they have no true north to guide them in making communication decisions.

Emotion is differentiating. Understand the set of values and emotions people want to tap into. One of the elements that makes Nike powerful is their understanding of the emotion inherent in all sports, coupled with the distinct emotional dynamics of each sport.

Be authentic. Consumers, across the board, can sense what is phony and contrived, and are on the lookout for fakeness. They don't connect with brands that are disingenuous.

Building Resonant Chambers

Real voice is not particularly loud. A pushy voice with a sharp edge is usually just as false as the whiny voice or the one that constantly apologizes for itself. All of these voices emanate from a shallower place than real voice. The distinction between real and false voices goes beyond motive or the place from which it begins; however, we can hear real voice in its impact on our ears—its timbre, resonance, distinctiveness, and authenticity.

Walk into any organization today, and it's easy to see where the chips are stacked. You see the office stars, the handful of people generating all of the ideas, clout, energy and drive. They know where they're going and the company lives off their firepower. But the rest of the office, the half-spirits, seem to become more listless and disengaged every time a full-spirit walks by. What an inefficient exchange of human resources!

How do we get the spirits on our team to become more real? How do we get every member of our team working as if it mattered? Sometimes they need more direction, more education, more incentives, better equipment, or more support, but the primary things that keep any of us from playing like stars are more internal. They are things like balance, energy, stamina, grace, and confidence, and the sense that we have something to bring to the conversation—and that when we bring it, we will be heard.

Resonance

The quality of a cello's sound is formed at the intersection of a player's skill and the resonance of the inner chamber of the instrument itself. An organization has the capacity to serve as a resonant cello chamber for its people, enhancing or diminishing their force and beauty by the resonance with which we surround them.

This "inner cello world or resonating chamber," is the defining discovery of Gilligan's recent work on voice. The people around us create an atmosphere that either encourages or distorts our capacity to give voice to our ideas. Keeping a chamber resonant requires mindfulness on everyone's part. It takes a long time to build, and can collapse in a moment.

We build resonance into our communities by speaking in our own real voices. It feels risky, especially because we know how easy it is to hit a wrong note—the clerk who's too perky, the boss who's too folksy, or the manager who's whiny. We're afraid we'll sound like them and it shuts us down. BUT, you do not sound like them! We have to trust our colleagues to recognize our real voices.

Building a resonant chamber means having confidence in both the speakers and the listeners within our organizations.

It also means asking second-layer questions. Gilligan has observed that people answer questions according to the level at which it is asked. They may answer a question one way the first time they are asked, and a completely different way the second time, even when the only variable is that they are being asked a second time.

For instance, a colleague tells you he cannot work with one of the managers in your office any longer because the guy's office is a mess and he can't bear walking by it. You listen, then say, "The mess really bugs you doesn't it? Is there anything else about it that gets to you?" He doubles back, "Actually, I don't mind the mess so much as I do the fact that he's always on the phone. He never even looks up to say hello when I walk by."

He's moved from a problem with the guy's messy office to his inattentiveness. A whole other dimension. They are related, but his second issue doesn't deny or expand on the first. Rather, the fact that you've listened longer and asked for more creates a new space, a less urgent and more expectant sounding board. What your colleague is saying is that the manager has made him feel less important than the business of his own desk. Before he says this to you, he may actually think the messy office is the problem. In asking him to say more you've asked him to think more, and to think in ways that resonate more deeply.

Because we live and talk at such multiple levels of meaning, sometimes all it takes to move one another to a different level is to ask again. And to know that the second answer doesn't give lie to the first, but acknowledges the multiplicity of our layered relationships to one another. Often we can establish a real voice relationship just by asking, *Can you help me understand this? Is there something I'm not getting? What would you do if the decision were yours to make?* Listening is the act of gathering; being heard is the act of being transformed. Everyone likes to be listened to; we fear—and long—to be heard. When we know we will be heard, we become smarter, truer, and more fully alive.

Listening to the Counterpoint

More than listening to the melody, choosing to pay attention to the counterpoint allows us to hear, not only the words of other groups and cultures, but the vast ineffable echoes of history and longing they bring with them. Welcoming them into our inner sanctum of true hearing, the place where we choose our reality.

If voice is the active choice to make one's mark upon the world, hearing is the choice to be marked by the voices of others. In many ways, we cannot avoid being affected by the voices of those around us. Sometimes they have a weathering or toughening effect on us that can actually dull our hearing, as when we are in a foreign country and become inured to the flow of language around us. After the initial shock — *they really do speak Portuguese in Portugal!* — we don't expect to understand anything.

When we hear other cultures only as one hears traffic or weather, we separate ourselves from it. We do the same thing when we find ourselves in situations we have no context for or expect to have no impact upon. We develop a sort of cultural autism. We can hear the sounds, but we can't imagine they have anything to do with us — or us with them so we tune them out. The alternative is to learn how to hear them.

Choosing to Hear across Cultures

In America we talk about *speaking* another language; in Kenya, they talk about *hearing* another language. The educated Kenyan will speak at least three languages: English, Swahili, and his own tribal language, but will be able to "hear" a variety of other tribal languages depending on where he grew up and where he has worked and gone to school. Maya Angelou, who has lived in Ghana and Europe, writes about the way that simply hearing another language stretches our capacity to conceive another way of being:

> The American, living in this vast country and able to traverse three thousand miles east to west using the same language, needs to hear languages as they collide in Europe, Africa, and Asia.

Angelou speaks seven languages fluently. She has an ear for several others. As she travels and talks with people across the world, she is always rolling the expressions and music of the languages she hears back into her own. She's currently working on a project in which she's writing children's stories for fifty different cultures—in their own languages.

When asked how she does it, she says, "I try. I learn them because I intend to. If I watch TV, I watch it in Spanish; I choose books to read in French. All of us can learn so much more than we realize. I choose to learn languages because I want to know people."

When We Listen Harder

Intentionality, curiosity, and risk-taking are essential to hearing another language, another culture, or another person. Over the last few years I've consciously become more active about *hearing* other cultures. What I'm realizing, of course, is how much I never heard, because I never thought it was about me.

In 1999 my physician husband and I returned to Kenya with our four teenage children for a six-month stint in a rural hospital. Not long after we arrived, we began caring for two orphans, Bui, whose mother had died in childbirth, and Joe, who had been found at three days old in a Nairobi marketplace—not an uncommon phenomenon on a continent where AIDS has orphaned 20 million children.

Through an amazing constellation of good will and good luck, we were able to adopt Bui and Joe, and to bring them back to America as our daughter and son. As you can imagine, the immediate reverberations for our household were significant. The dining room became Bui's bedroom, the kitchen was crowded with highchairs and bottles, and we're still finding old pacifiers under cushions.

For several months, issues of sleep and food overshadowed all else, but eventually larger issues began to make themselves known. We knew we were bringing Joe and Bui to our country, but we began to realize they would be taking us to a new country as well.

We recently heard Dr. Angelou speak at a wedding celebration. She said, "When we marry, we do not do so as individuals —we marry histories." Sometime during the chaotic first year of Joe and Bui's arrival, it struck us in adopting African children into a white American family, we had married histories. Our children, grandchildren, and great-grandchildren would grow up African-American in a world still skewed toward white privilege. If we expected them to grow up gracefully in such a world, the rest of our family needed to learn how to live gracefully in a black world.

We looked around and realized how little we knew. Our books, our classrooms, our neighborhood, and our church were mostly white. I couldn't even find hair products for Bui at my local pharmacy. We began to make changes wherever we could. We subscribed to *Oprah* and *Jet*, as well as *Time* and *Good Housekeeping*. We began visiting black churches, where we heard about black events and black speakers.

We had always known black individuals, but this was different. For the first time we were coming to know black people in a black context. We were beginning to hear history, politics, religion, and economics in a way we had never heard it before, and we began to realize how much we had missed. In writing this now, I take the risk of getting it wrong, and by the time you read it, I hope I'm hearing the African-American world better. But some of the lessons I'm learning are:

The goodwill extended toward a genuine learner is reward enough for the learner to continue listening.

We don't really begin to understand our own language until we begin to learn another one. What's more, our inability to read against the grain of our own culture renders us less intellectually effective in multiple fields.

If my beautiful five-year old brown-eyed Joe makes half the mistakes my three blue-eyed teen-age sons have made, he won't get away with it. And when he gets caught or tripped or tricked into whatever trouble a teenage boy is heir to, he will need a deep history of African-American faith, as well as the daily nourishment of his own faith, to bring him through the deadly dangers and temptations of racial discrimination.

Despite our bumper-to-bumper lives, we all miss hearing each other more often than not. I am making my own *lurch and learn* journey toward hearing a culture better. In making it, I've discovered a growing undercurrent of others who are suddenly aware of conversations they've missed all their lives— *Where was I when all this started? Why didn't I ever hear about this in school? Have we known about this for a long time?* We are hearing whole worlds of ideas for the first time, because we've chosen to. At the heart of our national cynicism about politically correct behavior and multicultural training are two issues:

A problem of delivery. Long before many of us had chosen to hear the real questions of cultural inequities, we have already been taught the answers. There is an over-abundance of supply-side political correctness, and too little hunger for trans-cultural understanding. Supply extinguishes demand. No curriculum or training workshop can substitute for the power of choice or hunger to know. We can all increase our own hunger for understanding—as well as the hunger of others, through independent and contagious acts of cross-cultural listening.

And a problem of conception. We protect ourselves from the work of learning real cultural theory by playing the "I" card, which protests: *Everyone is an individual and when we talk about gender, race, or culture we reduce individuals to types.* A comforting point of view, but it simply doesn't hold water. The truth is that as we learn more about the values and stories of cultures, we are more able to hear the individuals within them. We don't just hear individuals, we hear histories. Being able to imagine those histories, both as like and unlike our own, is the first unsettling step towards hearing them.

Choosing to Hear across Organizations

Research makes it clear that as business leaders move up the food chain, they change cultures and begin to speak a different language. They often lose their ability to hear, not just the feedback, but the real voices, longings, and languages that surround the actual work and exchange they are leading.

A CEO knows his company's vision statement, but he can't hear the roar of frustration and misfires that wash it out at the cash register. This hearing loss runs laterally too. What if the faculty of a university could hear the daily challenges of the admissions department? What if human resources knew what the new business division knows? What if management knew what maintenance knows? The often uncounted cost of power is the loss of easy access to hearing what we need to know.

Hearing the Bad News

The ways in which leaders have failed to hear bad news are epic — from George Custer to Arthur Anderson. Obviously all of us need to develop regular habits and trusted channels for hearing the things we don't want to know. Is my vision clear? Is my ego in check? Am I being distracted by non-essentials? Are my personal wounds undermining my leadership? Am I missing danger signals? Am I stepping on someone's baby? Am I delivering on my promises?

There is always bad news to be had, and little wonder we don't want to hear it. We will always disappoint some people. Both leaders and those they lead are caught in the gap between all of our hopes for a perfect leader and the flesh and blood real one we end up with. Together we must arrive at a continually renewable definition of "a good enough leader." As we learn to hear and give bad news as a part of the ongoing management of our own inevitable shortcomings and disappointments, the exchange becomes less toxic, more normal. Both sides of the management axis can take part in the process of creating a "good enough leader."

... And the Good

The value of learning to hear good news across levels of authority and divisions of responsibility, however, is as important as hearing the bad news. And it is hard to hear it across increasingly compartmentalized workplaces in the knowledge economy and the increasingly segmented society outside the workplace. To a great extent, contemporary society has traded in the shackles of patriarchal authority for the new tyranny of sibling rivalry. We no longer listen to the same music, wear the same clothes, or go to the same movies as one another. The downside of this is that a twenty-four year-old man may be speaking to the same problem that his forty-six year-old colleague is working on, but they are unable to draw on one another's draft because they don't realize they're going the same way.

Real hearing inevitably leads to change. And change is unsettling. But it is only through the work of unsettling that we ultimately make room for growth.

Unless we choose to do otherwise, we all miss so much more than we hear. However, when the speakers are brave, the chamber is resonant, and the melodies are rich and diverse, the cycle of hearing and speaking can be marvelously verdant—beyond anything we can grow in silence.

STATEMENT ON WOMEN AND MEN IN LEADERSHIP

Willow Creek Community Church

We believe the Bible teaches that men and women were created by God and equally bear his image (Genesis 1:27). God's intention was for them to share oneness and community (Genesis 2:23–24), even as the Godhead experiences oneness within the Trinity. Each had a direct relationship with God and they shared jointly the responsibilities of rearing children and having dominion over the created order (Genesis1:26–28). However, human oneness was shattered by the Fall. The struggle for power and the desire to "rule over" another is part of the result of human sin. Genesis 3:16 is a prediction of the effects of the Fall rather than a prescription of God's ideal order.

However, God has acted in Christ to redeem the human race, and to offer to all people the opportunity to be part of the New Community, his church. It is God's intention for his children to experience the oneness that exists between the Father and the Son

(John 17:11, 20–23). This means that old divisions and hierarchies between genders and races are not to be tolerated in the church, where all are "one in Christ Jesus" (Galatians 3:28).

In the formation of the church at Pentecost, the Holy Spirit was poured out on women and men alike, as had been predicted long before the coming of Christ (Joel 2:28; Acts 2:18). In the New Testament, women as well as men exercise prophetic and priestly functions (Acts 2:17–18; 1 Corinthians 11:4–5; 1 Peter 2:9–10). Further, the Spirit bestows gifts on all members of the New Community sovereignly, without giving anyone preferential treatment based on gender (Acts 2:1–21; 1 Corinthians 12:7, 11). Every believer is to offer her or his gifts for the benefit of the body of Christ (Romans 12:4–8; 1 Peter 4:10–11). To prevent believers from exercising their spiritual gifts is to quench the work of the Spirit.

In all attempts to understand and put into practice appropriate relationships between genders in the body of Christ, our sole authority is the will of God as expressed in Scripture. A few isolated scriptural texts appear to restrict the full ministry freedom of women. The interpretation of those passages must take into account their relation to the broader teaching of Scripture and their specific contexts. We believe that when the Bible is interpreted comprehensively, it teaches the full equality of men and women in status, giftedness, and opportunity for ministry.

Therefore, in our attempts to live together as a biblically functioning community, we are committed to the following values:

To provide opportunity for ministry based on giftedness and character, without regard to gender.

To pursue the kind of purity and loyalty in relationships between genders that led New Testament writers to describe them in terms of family: "brothers and sisters."

To use sensitivity in language that reflects the honor and value God desires for maleness and femaleness and to encourage the use of translations of Scripture that accurately portray God's will that his church be an inclusive community.

To be intentional where appropriate in overcoming sexist elements of our culture and to offer encouragement to women in areas where their giftedness has been traditionally discouraged.

To teach and model these values to members of our community, to the church, and to the world at large.

For further study and more complete discussion of the key scriptural passages pertaining to this issue, we recommend:

Beyond Sex Roles, Gilbert Bilezikian

Becoming a Woman of Strength, Ruth Haley Barton

Equal to Serve, Gretchen Hull

Paul, Women, Wives, Craig Keener

The New Reformation, Greg Ogden

Beyond the Curse, Aida Spencer

· APPENDIX 4 ·

FREQUENTLY ASKED QUESTIONS

1. **I have strong leadership gifts, but I'm married to a man who does not have leadership gifts. How does that work out in a marriage?**

This has been my experience. While my husband is described by those who know him as a person of strong influence and has led several different ministries in our church, he does not list leadership as one of his top gifts. Warren is highly analytical and strategic, and he processes information differently than I do. I am a quick thinker and often want to drive to decisions more quickly than he does. If I'm not careful, I can become manipulative in my leadership and "power up" in subtle ways to get what I want.

So how do we handle the belief many Christians hold that the husband is "the head of the home"? Does the man need to make the final call in all decisions for the family? I recognize there are varying points of view on this sensitive topic. Early in our marriage, I read the book *Heirs Together: Mutual Submission in Marriage*, by Patricia Gundry (Zondervan, 1980). I believe both husbands and wives are called to submit to one another in Christ. In our marriage, Warren and I strive to listen to one another and come to consensus on decisions we face. Our everyday reality does not include the idea of one of us always winning or making the final call. Rather, we seek to decide together after listening to the Holy

Spirit and to each other's point of view. I honestly can't recall a single time when Warren has said, "I'm the husband, the head of the home, and therefore this is the way it's going to be."

Being married to someone who is not a natural leader has been challenging for me. I must regularly submit first and foremost to the work of the Spirit in my life in order to exhibit characteristics such as humility, gentleness, kindness, and self-control. Warren has helped me grow spiritually by holding me accountable if I start to degenerate into manipulation or conniving. Learning these lessons in my home also informs my leadership in ministry, with individuals who also do not define themselves as leaders.

2. I am a young woman just beginning to lead in the church. How different do you think my reality is from the issues you faced ten or fifteen years ago?

Certainly each situation is unique, but my impression is that while some progress has been made for women to fully express their gifts, we still have a long way to go in most churches. Generally, church cultures take a long time to see significant change, especially when it comes to issues about which faithful people hold to different interpretations of Scripture and where traditions have been held tightly for a long time. I rejoice that there are some vibrant churches in which men and women are free to lead and teach without any big deal being made about it—whoever has the gifts and is affirmed can minister fully.

If you are just beginning to get involved in a church, I encourage you to make careful observations of the opportunities afforded to women. In addition, be sure to investigate any written policies about gender and leadership for that particular church and/or its denomination. In some churches, the reality does not match the written policies. Also observe the teaching at your church. How are issues of women in leadership addressed, if at all, and how are women described and spoken to by the male teachers and leaders? Do women lead and teach the congregation as a whole, or are they limited to teaching other women and/or children? Do any women lead men who work on staff or as volunteers?

Gandhi is often quoted as having said, "Be the change you want to see in the world." My challenge to you as a young woman leader is to seize any opportunity to lead or teach in your church, no matter what the size of the team or audience, and to model authenticity, grace, wisdom, character, and excellence in all that you do. May God open whatever doors can be opened for you, and may others (men and women) see it as a no-brainer for you to lead and teach!

3. **A man who reports to me often displays resistance to my leadership. How should I handle this?**

Ideally, these difficult situations can be avoided if leaders at the top clearly communicate a church's policy about women in leadership before anyone is hired and accepts a staff or volunteer role. In our church, the elders include conversation about our affirmation of men and women leaders in each interview of potential staff. If a person cannot respectfully submit to a woman leader, or receive teaching from a woman, he or she is not hired. Clarifying expectations up front is best.

But in many situations, these conversations do not take place, and some churches face awkward transitions as more women assume roles that were previously filled by men. In the day-to-day reality of doing ministry, the deeply held convictions about how to interpret difficult Scripture passages, as well as the traditions many grew up with, result in friction and resentment. The first step to take is to bring "the elephant in the room" out into the open and have a conversation with the man who is resistant. Give him the opportunity to explore with you why he behaves as he does, and actively listen to him. Chances are good that he has had experiences in the past that have formed his point of view and perhaps even turned him against women in leadership roles. You will need to lean into the support of your own leaders if the man stays stuck, and potentially invite a third party (either your supervisor or an elder) into the dialogue if that becomes necessary. If this is a situation with a staff person, I advise you to document the essence of these conversations in writing.

My experience has been that most men who struggle with a woman leader are responsive to changing their point of view when they begin to see their worst fears do not have to come true. When you show the men on your team that you are for them, that you are not a power-hungry or angry woman with an agenda, most of the time they will give you a chance. For the few who simply will not open their minds or their hearts, recognize that this is not really about you individually, but more about an overall point of view which they may be totally unwilling to adjust. In that case, the leaders above you will hopefully support you, and the man will need to transition off the team. He may even decide he cannot continue as a participating member of your church because of the difference in his point of view.

4. **How important are job titles? Is it worth it to lobby for the same titles men have who carry out similar roles?**

I have heard of situations in which a woman does the same job as a man on a church team, but cannot hold the title of pastor or minister, so she is called a director or given some other title. At the risk of seeming "small," I think titles do matter. People hold perceptions of a person's role and responsibilities based on these titles, and may assume a woman does not have leadership authority if her title is distinctly different from men in similar positions.

Titles, salary decisions, and office locations are all triggers that allow a church team to wrestle with the deeper issue of women in leadership and women teaching. When a title needs to be announced, or a salary level decided, or an office provided, we discover what we really believe about gender and the rubber meets the road. Therefore, these practical issues (which, of course, all of us wish to be perceived as not so important) propel us, if we are wise, into profound conversations that we simply must have. If a church is moving toward a more egalitarian view of women in leadership, change will take time — and some of those changes may prove exceedingly difficult to execute. Senior leaders will discover if they really mean what they say on these policies when they are forced to make decisions about such practical issues as titles.

In churches that hold a more conservative or traditional view, titles may continue to be different according to gender. A woman who holds the same responsibilities as a man doing the same job (and possibly being paid less) will have to work extra hard to serve with joy and humility. Ask yourself regularly if this is what God is calling you to do. If this is what you feel called to do, God will give you the grace to be faithful no matter what. But don't continue in the situation out of fear of asking the tough questions. Maybe you are the person God will use as an agent of change.

5. **How can I possibly fit it all in — ministry responsibilities, exercise, time with family, household management, time with friends, solitude, and everyday stuff like getting the oil changed in the car and going to the dentist?!**

My husband and I often joke with one another that we are one adult short in our home and desperately need either a butler or a maid. If all of us added up the hours required to do everything we know we "should" do every week, none of us would get any sleep (and experts tell us we're supposed to have eight hours of shut-eye). So much of managing our lives begins with adjusting our expectations and not being too hard on ourselves, especially in certain seasons of life.

The hardest year of our marriage schedule-wise was the first year after the birth of our second daughter. With a four-year-old and a baby, my husband and I could not figure out how to do ministry and life without losing our minds. One day we realized that somewhere along the way, we had "gotten off the same team." The precious few minutes of discretionary time either of us had fostered resentment in the other person: "Why did you get to work out when I haven't had the chance all week?" "How come you got to get together with your friends and I haven't had the chance?" To show just how pathetic this became, I remember walking extra slowly at the grocery store while Warren was home with the kids, just because I so desperately needed some time alone.

Once we recognized how absurd we were becoming, and how neither of us were really "winning" with this kind of sick behavior, we had an honest conversation and determined to get back on the same team. We decided to become advocates for one another, so that hopefully both of us could "win" at least some of the time. Every so often, we pulled out our calendars to talk through our schedules. Warren still dreads our "calendar meetings," but he knows that if we don't have those conversations, both of us will overcommit and our lives will be totally unmanageable.

You may want to periodically reread chapter 5, and remind yourself that none of us can have it all ... all at once. I have made countless adjustments over the years for the cleanliness standards of my home, for how often I can see friends, for how much I can contribute time to my daughters' schools and other volunteer activities. If you are single or married without children, your life is also complex and difficult to manage, though your specific challenges may be different. And for single moms, I can only say that you are heroic in my book, and I hope you give yourself grace at every turn.

6. I am part of a church (and denomination) in which the position on women leaders teaching is more conservative. What steps can I take to urge church leaders to revisit that position? Or should I give up and find another church in which I can serve freely?)

At the end of chapter 2 (pages 43–45), I describe the advice I would give a woman in a similar dilemma. I will add just a few thoughts to that material here.

Nothing ever changes unless godly people are willing to engage in the difficult conversations that lead to change. Of course, these conversations require courage and time. I encourage you to first do your homework. Make sure you fully understand your church's position on gender and the leadership/teaching gifts. In order to be certain you have the full picture, this requires both looking at any written policies and exploring what really happens in the day-to-day trenches of ministry. In most situations, a church culture is highly affected by the senior pastor's personal views as well, so be sure you clearly understand that individual's point of view.

Once you have done your homework, begin the process of inviting dialogue by asking the appropriate people if they would be open to meeting with you. Depending on your unique situation, this may include elders or deacons as well as senior staff members and, of course, the senior pastor. Ask good questions in order to discern the accuracy of your impressions of the church's position. For example, investigate what limits, if any, exist for women with leadership and teaching gifts by proposing a hypothetical situation: "Could there ever be a woman serving as the senior pastor at this church, or as an elder or as an associate pastor?" Then ask whether there is any openness to revisiting those policies, beginning with a study of some books or other resources to explore various viewpoints and interpretations of Scripture. A good starting point might be to listen to John Ortberg's four-part message series, "What the Bible Says about Men and Women" (see Additional Resources, page 182). Perhaps you could assemble a package of key chapters from some books, and read through chapter 7 from this book.

Prepare yourself for a long journey. In most churches this process—from opening up dialogue to initiating actual change—takes many months, if not years. Ask the Holy Spirit to give you the discernment to know when you need to keep moving the process along, and when you need to back off for a time. Obviously, you will want to display the character that consistently "speaks the truth in love" and avoids harsh or slanderous talk along the way.

God may use you as a catalyst for change in your church and possibly even in your denomination. Or you may end up completely frustrated and make no progress at all. At any point, the Spirit may free you up to transition to a church where the battle is not so hard. No one can tell you what path God has for you, but I cheer you on and know you will be blessed as you seek to listen for God's voice and to courageously obey what you hear.

7. I have a young daughter who shows signs of being a leader. What advice would you give me?

No matter what gifts our children display, we must affirm those gifts and help our children to develop them. Look in your daughter's eyes and tell her what you see in her. Name the gift of leadership or teaching and let her know she is blessed by God to be entrusted with those gifts. Seize any opportunities you have day-to-day to observe your daughter's abilities in action, and then communicate to her what you see: "I noticed how you treated your friends today at your birthday party, and how you tried so hard to include everyone. That was good leadership!" As she gets older, you can also help her understand that these gifts come with tremendous responsibility.

Much has been written about how parents tend to socialize sons and daughters differently, and how that ultimately affects their career choices and behavior. I delight in how we are learning that young girls can excel in sports (as my girls do) and can gravitate toward the sciences or politics or any field they choose. Your daughter needs to see women leading in a variety of settings. It may be wise for you to intentionally choose a female pediatrician, or a female athletic coach. If your church does not have women in visible leadership or teaching roles, occasionally take your daughter to visit a church that does. You will be vision-casting! Allow her to dream about all kinds of possibilities for ways she could express her gifts in the future.

Train your daughter carefully (without bitterness) to recognize when girls are being treated differently than boys and when it is unfair. You can do this by watching television together and pointing out certain stereotypes, or looking at a magazine and learning about how girls are expected to conform to an unrealistic body image. Initiate conversations with your daughter about how she contributes in class at school, and whether she ever tries to mask her intelligence or abilities. Expose your daughter to biographies of outstanding women in a variety of fields to offer her many models for inspiration.

When my girls showed interest and abilities in the area of the arts, I began to talk with them more often about what I experienced day-to-day as a leader of an arts team. After church services, I encouraged dialogue with them about what we experienced, trying to develop their instincts for what engaged the congregation and what seemed to miss. We frequently attend professional theatrical productions so we can be inspired and learn by example. I also ask my daughters to give me feedback whenever I teach, so I can benefit from their input and develop their own communication skills.

If your daughter's father is still living and engaged in her life, he has an enormous role in helping to form your daughter's self-image and confidence. I love to watch my husband coach my daughters in sports because he calls out an entirely different side of them and encourages healthy competition and aggressiveness.

It can be so difficult as a parent to avoid our controlling tendencies and not attempt to squeeze our children into some kind of mold. I try not to make assumptions about my daughters' futures. They may or may not get married someday, and they may or may not become mothers themselves. I want them to know that their lives can be abundantly full and deeply satisfying no matter what the circumstances turn out to be.

The best thing you can do, of course, is model what godly leadership looks like. None of us does this perfectly, but whenever your daughter sees you in action, when she sees your passion and stewardship of your own gifts, when she understands that your entire life and joy are not connected to motherhood (though that is huge), then she will be more and more free to become all that God has in mind for her. Let her know when you make mistakes, when you get out of balance, even times when you feel frustrated. She doesn't need to see you as a superstar, only as a woman doing the very best she can. And one day (so I'm told), she will rise up and call you blessed!

◆ Notes ◆

1. Anna Fels, *Necessary Dreams* (New York: Pantheon, 2004), 193.
2. Dr. Henry Cloud, *Integrity* (New York: HarperCollins, 2006), 8.
3. Amy Poehler, quoted in Maureen Ryan, "Tina Fey's climb to the top of the comedy heap," *Chicago Tribune*, September 30, 2007.
4. Anna Fels, *Necessary Dreams* (New York: Pantheon, 2004), 19.
5. Dr. Sarah Sumner, *Men and Women in the Church* (Downers Grove: InterVarsity, 2003), 74.
6. Melinda M. Marshall, *Good Enough Mothers* (Princeton, N.J.: Peterson's, 1993), 91.
7. Marshall, *Good Enough Mothers*, 47.
8. Donna St. George, "Hey, Mom, you are doing fine, study says," *Chicago Tribune*, March 21, 2007.
9. Dr. Henry Cloud and Dr. John Townsend, *Boundaries with Kids* (Grand Rapids: Zondervan, 1998), 117.
10. Jane Stephens, "The Rhetoric of Women's Leadership: Language, Memory, and Imagination," *Journal of Leadership and Organizational Studies* 9, no. 3 (2003): 45–60.
11. Jane Stephens and Stephen Zades, *Mad Dogs, Dreamers, and Sages: Growth in the Age of Ideas* (New York: Elounda Press, 2003), 92.
12. Stephens and Zades, *Mad Dogs*, 94.
13. Frederick Buechner, *Now and Then* (San Francisco: Harper & Row, 1983), 87, 92.
14. Parker Palmer, *The Courage to Teach: Exploring the Inner Landscape of a Teacher's Life* (San Francisco: Jossey-Bass, 1998), 17.
15. Craig Blomberg, *Two Views on Women in Ministry* (Grand Rapids: Zondervan, 2005), 123.
16. Dan Kimball, *They Like Jesus but Not the Church* (Grand Rapids: Zondervan, 2007), 115.
17. Dr. Lois P. Frankel, *See Jane Lead* (New York: Warner Business, 2007), 20.
18. Frankel, *See Jane Lead*, 20.
19. Betsy Cohen, *The Snow White Syndrome* (New York: Macmillan, 1986), 41.
20. As quoted in Betsy Cohen, *The Snow White Syndrome* (New York: Macmillan, 1986), 17.
21. As quoted in Cohen, *Snow White Syndrome*, 234.

22. Lynne Hybels, *Nice Girls Don't Change the World* (Grand Rapids: Zondervan, 2005), 86.

23. Lynette Lewis, *Climbing the Ladder in Stilettos* (Nashville: Thomas Nelson, 2006), 158.

ABOUT THE AUTHOR

Nancy Beach is a speaker, author, visionary leader, and champion for the power of the arts and artists in the local church. She served for more than twenty years as the programming director for Willow Creek Community Church in suburban Chicago, a congregation known around the world for creating culturally relevant, biblically based services that make full use of the arts.

Dedicated to creating opportunities for artists in the church to use their gifts for effective ministry, her role at Willow Creek included leadership of all aspects of the arts — worship, music, drama, dance, photography, production, video, and design. Today, Nancy continues her role as a teaching pastor at Willow Creek while also serving as the executive vice president for the arts at the Willow Creek Association, a not-for-profit organization serving over 12,000 member churches and others, representing over ninety denominations in thirty-five countries. This responsibility allows her to focus the majority of her time on serving other church arts leaders and their teams in the United States and around the world, building a community of Christ-following artists seeking to serve God as they create transformational moments in Sunday morning church services.

A sought-after conference speaker, Nancy uses her teaching gifts to inspire, motivate, and cast vision, while skillfully relating themes of spiritual transformation with everyday people and experiences. Her first book, *An Hour on Sunday*, expresses Nancy's core vision and values for effective arts ministries.

Nancy and her husband, Warren, live in the Chicago suburbs with their two teenage daughters and a cat named Elphaba.

An Hour on Sunday

Creating Moments of Transformation and Wonder

Nancy Beach

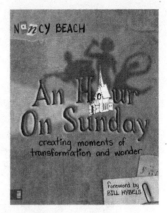

Today's spiritually searching culture is less inclined than ever to attend church. Yet, no time of the week is filled with more life-changing potential than Sunday morning.

Imagine . . .

- experiences that bring people heart-to-heart with God.
- messages in which God's truth connects to everyday life.
- transcendent moments that leave people awestruck—and transformed.

That's what can happen when you unleash the arts in your church through the power of the Holy Spirit. *An Hour on Sunday* is not about nitty-gritty programming details or cookie-cutter how-to's. It's about foundational issues—ten enduring principles that:

- unite artists and ministry leaders around a common language
- empower artists and pastors to effectively work together, and
- create the potential for moments that matter on Sunday morning.

An Hour on Sunday is for worship and arts ministry leaders, pastors and teachers, artists—including musicians, writers, dancers, actors, visual artists, film makers, light and sound engineers—and anyone who believes in the limitless potential of the arts in their church.

Whimsically illustrated, written with passion and humor, and filled with stories of both success and failure, *An Hour on Sunday* explores the deep, shaping forces that can make your hour on Sunday a time of transformation and wonder for believers and seekers alike.

Jacketed Hardcover: 978-0-310-25296-2

Pick up a copy today at your favorite bookstore!

WILLOW
Willow Creek Association

Willow Creek Association
Vision, Training, Resources for Prevailing Churches

This resource was created to serve you and to help you build a local church that prevails. It is just one of many ministry tools that are part of the Willow Creek Resources® line, published by the Willow Creek Association together with Zondervan.

The Willow Creek Association (WCA) was created in 1992 to serve a rapidly growing number of churches from across the denominational spectrum that are committed to helping unchurched people become fully devoted followers of Christ. Membership in the WCA now numbers over 12,000 Member Churches worldwide from more than ninety denominations.

The Willow Creek Association links like-minded Christian leaders with each other and with strategic vision, training, and resources in order to help them build prevailing churches designed to reach their redemptive potential. Here are some of the ways the WCA does that.

- **The Leadership Summit**—A once a year, two-day learning experience to envision and equip Christians with leadership gifts and responsibilities. Presented live at Willow Creek as well as via satellite broadcast to over 135 locations across North America, this event is designed to increase the leadership effectiveness of pastors, ministry staff, volunteer church leaders, and Christians in the marketplace.

- **Ministry-Specific Conferences**—Throughout each year the WCA hosts a variety of conferences and training events—both at Willow Creek's main campus and offsite, across North America and around the world. These events are for church leaders and volunteers in areas such as group life, children's ministry, student ministry, preaching and teaching the arts and stewardship.

- **Willow Creek Resources®**—Provides churches with trusted and field-tested ministry resources on important topics such as leadership, volunteer ministries, spiritual formation, stewardship, evangelism, group life, children's ministry, student ministry, the arts, and more.

- **WCA Member Benefits**—Includes substantial discounts to WCA training events, a 20 percent discount on all Willow Creek Resources®, *Defining Moments* monthly audio journal for leaders, quarterly *Willow* magazine, access to a Members-Only section on the WCA's web site, monthly communications, and more. Member Churches also receive special discounts and premier services through WCA's growing number of ministry partners—Select Service Providers—and save an average of $500 annually depending on the level of engagement.

For specific information about WCA conferences, resources, membership, and other ministry services contact:

Willow Creek Association
P.O. Box 3188, Barrington, IL 60011-3188
Phone: 847-570-9812, Fax: 847-765-5046

www.willowcreek.com